"Emilie A. Frank's inspiri **USE ONLY** California's Mystic Mountain,"
is destined to be a classic ~~Overflowing with~~ spiritual inspiration, legend,
and lore from beautiful Mt. Shasta. Emilie has finally brought into print a
much needed metaphysical map for seekers around the world about this
enchanting and passionate vortex. Her extensive research and entertaining
approach to writing will fill your senses. One thing for sure, this book will
bring you hours of literary joy!!!"
Diana Chapman, owner, "Wings Bookstore," Mt. Shasta, California

"As a writer and a long time Mt. Shasta resident, I spend a lot of my time.
climbing Mt. Shasta always keeping in mind the mysticism, legends, and
lore that surround this majestic volcano. Unbelievably, I read this book in
one evening and found it to be the most complete book ever written on the
mysteries of Mt. Shasta. This book will truly be a companion in my back-
pack (as it should be yours)."
Steve Lewis, author of *Climbing Mt. Shasta,* Mt. Shasta, California

"This is the book, I am sure, that many have been waiting for. It is truly vin-
tage Emilie Frank."
Cindy Schultheis-Melberg, *Supersaver Advertiser*

"At last, a professional, comprehensive, intriguing book about Mt. Shasta.
Our Mystic Mountain will be seen in a new light... thank you Emilie."
Jim Martin, retired, publisher of *Supersaver Advertiser* for 18 years, friend and admir-
er, Mt. Shasta, California

"Emilie Frank gathered and wrote in a straightforward manner the best possible analysis of the various mystical legends about Mt. Shasta. A most
readable reference work for those interested in this aspect of this spectacular
mountain."
Or Apperson, retired, owner for 38 years of the *Mt. Shasta Herald* newspaper, and
lifelong resident of Mt. Shasta, California

Mt. Shasta

California's

Mystic Mountain

Emilie A. Frank

PHOTOGRAFIX
Publishing

Hilt,
California

Dedication

We dedicate

the publication of this book

to our mother's memory.

In honor of her hard work

as a freelance writer for

Siskiyou County

and author of this book.

With Love,
Dana
David
Paula
Jennifer

Acknowledgements

I would like to thank **PhotograFix Publishing Services** for helping to create a book that our family will always be proud of.

To **Kevin Cornwell**, who truly went the extra mile, "never lose sight of those ocean sunsets that await your sails."

Jacquie Cornwell, thank you for your photographic restoration and literary talents — your opinions were greatly appreciated.

To all the **photographers**, many of which were personal friends, family, and cohorts of Emilie's, thank you for so graciously contributing to the interest and beauty of this book.

Valarie Landis for her editing skills. At the last, she opened her schedule to edit the manuscript. I enjoyed your positive contributions and warm encouragement.

Don Middleton, the energy it took to create this book took time away from you, the house, and the kitchen. As usual, and without complaint, you have been a champ, thanks hon, I love you.

For all their reviews on such short notice, a sincere thank you to: **Diana Chapman**, Wings Bookstore; **Steve Lewis**, Author *Climbing Mt. Shasta;* **Cindy Schultheis-Melberg**, *Supersaver Advertiser;* **Jim Martin**, retired publisher, *Supersaver Advertiser;* **Or Apperson**, retired publisher, *Mt. Shasta Herald*.

And especially our late mother, **Emilie A. Frank**, whose work is reflected in the pages of this book. Her untiring research and countless hours of study about Mt. Shasta has given us this manuscript, an unparalleled heirloom. Her spirit now resides with the mountain.

Jennifer Middleton

Foreword

Go to India and a guru will tell you to go to Mt. Shasta. Interview local mystics and they'll tell you fascinating stories about having been inside golden temples deep inside Mt. Shasta.

Read any number of books on the subject of Mt. Shasta and discover tales beyond your imagination, weird legends about a supernatural race called Lemurians who escaped to the mountain after their continent sank into the depths of what is now known as the Pacific Ocean. Or about another race of supernatural dwarfs who dwell in caves, or about survivors of the lost continent of Atlantis who reportedly live in a wondrous city deep within Mt. Shasta, the splendor of which would be indescribable.

Oh, the stories that have been told about her...

Her? Yes, her.

Of course, poet Joaquin Miller called Mt. Shasta "him" but he was wrong. Would he have called America "him" or a battleship, or the Grand Old Flag?

But Joaquin Miller did call Mt. Shasta "the most comely and perfect snowpeak in America" and he did describe her as being "white and flashing like a pyramid of silver" and yes, it was he who said Mt. Shasta was "lonely as God and white as a winter moon." So we forgive you, Joaquin Miller, for using the wrong gender.

As for me, I moved to Mt. Shasta's quiet slopes many moons ago because I fell under her spell while passing through the area. She was white and shining. I was bedazzled. Why wouldn't I be? I was a native of Illinois, that flat midwestern prairieland and had never before seen such glory.

Before me, that golden October day, rose majestically the most spectacular sight. A lone, snow-covered, glistening mountain rising 14,162-feet into an azure sky, with a curious lenticular cloud hovering above her peak. And drifting about her and toward her were many more white silver-dollar-like lenticular clouds, just as though they were there for a reason. (And there are those, I found out later, who say the lenticulars are there for a reason.)

Within a month I was back with all my earthly belongings to live on her slopes forevermore, to dwell in the beauty of her mighty presence. At that time I was completely unaware of her mysteries. Now, many years later, I would like to tell her story.

Mt. Shasta. Poets have heralded this mountain since her discovery in the year 1786 when a French explorer sailed along the northwestern coast of what is now California and wrote in his log that he was only four leagues from shore and that he "perceived a volcano on the summit of the mountain which bore east of us, its flame very likely, but thick fog soon concealed it from our sight." It is thought by some historians that Jean de La Perouse was witnessing an eruption of Mt. Shasta.

Writers have written reams about her. Artists have immortalized her. Newspapers and magazines have sent innumerable reporters and feature writers to her slopes to look for those reported mysterious bells and gold-lined caverns and supernatural beings, both large and small. And to interview psychics and mystics who live nearby.

And when I, as a writer, was asked over the years if the legends and mysterious tales about Mt. Shasta were true, I always said that I didn't know and tried to change the subject.

Why? Well, how could I ever explain the group who visited my home one summer evening and told me about their breathtaking experience on the slopes of Mt. Shasta when they chanced upon a "being" they claimed was the former Queen of Lemuria?

And how could I possibly explain a taped interview with another very psychic young lady in which I was told that Lemurian beings actually materialized one New Year's Day in the very room in which we were sitting? That she had seen them and had communicated with them.

Mysteries. Many, many mysteries. Mt. Shasta is an ancient mountain and like all landmarks birthed in antiquity, she is the progenitor of myths and legends and mysterious happenings. She has been this writer's dream, always turning up yet another mystery if I dig deeply into museums and obscure books. Or prod shadowy people who have eerie experiences to tell.

And then I ponder the sacred mountain — and it is considered to be sacred by many — anew. I realize that I am still completely awed by this white, mystic mountain and always have been. Nothing anywhere can equal the beauty and the otherworldly occult charm of Mt. Shasta. Of that I am sure.

One small detail should be explained and that is why this mountain is referred to as Mt. Shasta and not Mount Shasta. Simply because writers in the area always use the abbreviated form in order to distinguish the mountain itself from the small village of Mount Shasta, which is a ski resort and lies on the mountain's lower southern slopes.

Often silhouetted against a rose-tinged sky, Mt. Shasta stands alone and silent. This enchanting mountain has always been enshrouded in mystery and those who are aware of her legends observe her glacier-carved upper slopes with wonder.

She is California's mystic mountain, was ever thus, and I feel privileged that it was my destiny to record the following collection of wonderful and often astonishing legends, a collection (gathered over a period of 20 years) which includes strange interviews and incredible, fanciful tales about this historic sentinel of northern California.

Emilie A. Frank
Mount Shasta, California
October, 1992

photo by Bobbie Richardson

Contents

The Lady on The Mountain

In repose on top of the mountain, the legendary Lady on the Mountain can be most easily seen while traveling on Interstate 5 between Dunsmuir and Mt. Shasta City. Her features are clearly defined during the winter months when Mt. Shasta is heavily cloaked in snow. Sketch by Jennifer Middleton.

Chapter 1

The Mt. Shasta Mystique

Have you ever seen a more

beautiful mountain?

Rising

white and solitary and serene,

this mighty sentinel

guards her kingdom,

as always.

High in the mist and sealed throughout the ages in ice and snow, the ancient volcano that is Mt. Shasta is wondrous to behold — a glittering, enchantment. An awesome mountain, sacred to many.

For over a hundred years psychic souls have been writing strange things about this shining peak which rises in solitary splendor, 14,162 feet into northern California's blue sky. Perennially blanketed in white, Mt. Shasta appears to be serene. She is serene. She is immutably silent. And heavily permeated in mystery — myriads of mysteries.

Her fame has spread to India, to China, to Peru, and seers in other far-off lands will tell you that mystery and intrigue have always been synonymous with this great landmark.

Mystery and intrigue, indeed. Would you believe secret caverns lined with gold? Strange lights on her slopes? Golden domes, ringing bells, supernatural beings? Ancient Lemurian gold mines? Cities ten miles beneath her crest?

Many summer suns have witnessed all manner of "happenings" and many winter moons have transformed this mystic mountain into a luminous white shrine. A shrine sometimes enhanced by strange lenticular clouds which hover just above her snowy peak — creating, of course, even more peculiar tales that spaceships hide in those odd, circular cloud-formations and that Mt. Shasta is one of their fueling sites.

If that sounds outrageous, let me state that more than one person living on the slopes of Shasta have seen spaceships.

Mt. Shasta is also a vast playground for travelers who ski its slopes during the winter or climb to her crest during the summer months, and that's why it seems paradoxical that so few of them realize that this mountain is as sacred as Sinai to many mystical sects and cults all over the world.

It's true. Very few visitors photographing the mountain realize that ethereal beings possessing supernatural powers are reputed to dwell beneath her mighty flanks. And maybe it's just as well...

Still, many books have been written about this western peak and the strange goings-on, and these writings have, in turn, attracted metaphysicians, parapsychologists, seers, mediums, and other mystics to her slopes. And they, too, wonder about the stories. Is there really a beautiful city, or cities, inhabited by advanced civilizations ten miles beneath this snowy mountain? And if there are, are these cities inhabited by Lemurians, survivors of the lost continent of Lemuria (Mu), or are they inhabited, as some claim, by a colony of Atlanteans, survivors of the lost continent of Atlantis?

Is there really a marble and gold temple inside Mt. Shasta, as has been written, where Phylos the Tibetan comes to teach a chosen few? And what about that prospector operating under the alias of J. C. Brown who claimed to have discovered within the mountain a great cavern upon whose walls hung golden plates and shields engraved with strange drawings and hieroglyphics? And the cavern floor, he wrote in his journal, was littered with the skeletons of a giant, prehistoric race.

Then there is the mystery of the bells — an extraordinary legend which discloses that the mountain is inhabited by Yaktavians who are reported to be the greatest bell makers in the world. This is one of the most fascinating mysteries concerning Mt. Shasta and was recorded under the title "California Bell Legends: A Survey" in the *California Folklore Quarterly* published by the University of California in Los Angeles, Vol. IV, No. 1, January, 1945.

"According to the initiated," the publication states, "the greatest bells in the universe are the bells of the Secret Commonwealth in the great cities of Iletheleme and Yaktavia which lie deep in the vast mass of Mt. Shasta. The Yaktavians are said to be the greatest bell makers in the world and for tone and musical sound their bells cannot be surpassed." They reputedly built their underground cities with bells, that is, they hollowed out the vast area beneath the mountain with the sound of bells and mighty chimes, the sound vibrations moving enormous masses of debris and rock.

Furthermore, it is said the constant and continuous sound of bells illuminate their great halls, corridors, and tunnels, by vibrating atoms of ether in such a way as to promote light.

According to the legend, the Yaktavians, in order to insure their privacy, erected a great bell made of transparent material on the northwest side of the mountain — material which reflects no light and is invisible beyond 18 inches. The wind, striking the lip of this bell, causes a sound so high-pitched and of such peculiar vibration that it repels would-be trespassers on the holy ground that surrounds the entrance to the Secret Commonwealth.

There is more to this legend. On stretches of the forest roads leading to the upper slopes of the mountain, bells are reputedly heard — great booming bell sounds or crashing chime sounds — and that sometimes travelers' automobiles stop dead and can not be started again until the bells cease to ring. But the legend also says that persons lost on the slopes of Mt. Shasta have been mercifully guided to safety by following the bell sounds.

The secret would seem to lie in the first four words of the bell legend article, "According to the initiated." But the bell legend is just one of many obscure mysteries relating to Mt. Shasta which have come down through the corridors of time.

There are mountains and mountains, to be sure, but what other mountain is said to secrete within her bosom several cities carved by bells? What other mountain is said to harbour within, the survivors of Lemuria and Atlantis? And are there really shafts of gold leading to subterranean mines, and is there a world within, a world containing treasure vaults of yet another civilization, still there, exactly as they were left after 'whatever' happened to those prehistoric inhabitants?

Enveloped in beauty, as always, Mt. Shasta beams benevolently down on alpine lakes, on forests which stretch endlessly as far as the eye can behold, on cool canyons wherein whitewater rivers flow in relative obscurity. She seems unaware that earth-bound mortals wonder about her mysteries, that she is one of the seven sacred mountains in the world.

photo courtesy Ed Stockton

Chapter 2

The Lemurians

The theory

that Mt. Shasta is inhabited

by Lemurians

has been contradicted.

Dr. M. Doreal contends

the mountain is inhabited

by Atlanteans in

underground cities.

Since the fabled Lemurians will be "materializing" in many of the legends, stories, and interviews included in this book, let us delve into their origin first because these survivors of the lost continent of Lemuria are reputed (by many) to be living in supernatural form deep within Mt. Shasta. And because there are intertwining stories about the Lemurians — that is, they not only seem to dominate all the other "beings" connected with Mt. Shasta, they are also sometimes involved in other legends.

I have found, during twenty years of research, that the Lemurians have unexpectedly materialized (I know no other word) in many obscure books and other odd literature that I have run across throughout the years. Not to mention the very unusual interviews I have had with local men and women in which Lemurians have been heavily involved.

The famous story of the Lemurians inhabiting Mt. Shasta is known all over the world, and it is said that the entire western coast of the United States is supposedly the remains of the continent of Lemuria. Even disbelievers cannot dispute the fact that the mountainous terrain on the west coast is indeed different. The cataclysmic action that caused the submersion of Lemuria is said to have also caused the now-continent of North America to rise from its partially submerged state, join with the mountainous remnant of Lemuria, and thus form the continent which was later named North America.

In 1931 a fascinating book entitled *Lemuria — The Lost Continent of the Pacific* was published, written by Wishar S. Cerve. He said he was a student of archaeology, geology, and meteorology and that he spent ten years in research. He also had at his disposal many ancient manuscripts and maps. Deciding to gather together the thousands of recorded facts and the vast collection from all over the world of reports, legends, and findings regarding Lemuria he put them into book form because he believed that all the races of man throughout the world as we know it had one common origin, the Lemurians. And that environment and climate changed their nature, habits, and appearance. Cerve emphatically believed that Mt. Shasta was the last refuge of the survivors of the lost continent of Lemuria.

The book was very widely read, and, shortly after it was published, searchers for the Lemurian colony inside Mt. Shasta came from all over the world. Letters of inquiry poured into the offices of the local United States Forest Service, and all were officially answered. What's more, Forest Service personnel claimed that they searched the entire mountain and the surrounding flats and that the mountain was photographed from the air. After a while the United States Forest Service dutifully reported that no one had ever encountered a Lemurian.

Nevertheless, many still believed that the author presented his facts in such a way that it did seem reasonable that part of California was once the eastern coast of Lemuria.

According to Cerve, two hundred thousand years ago the surface of the earth was much different than it is today: North America, Europe, Africa, South America and Asia were joined and much of this land was either submerged beneath water or it was a form of swampland and uninhabitable. And as long ago as 150,000 years, he states, these partially submerged lands were known and described and sometimes pictured on crude and ancient maps.

Prehistoric people, he wrote, lived on the continent of Lemuria, also called Mu. This extremely ancient continent was supposedly the cradle of the human race, and on it was the Garden of Eden. (It seems, Cerve states, that in all ancient records and among all ancient tribes there is a trace of this same story of the creation of man in a Garden of Eden, and the earliest records indicate that man was created co-incident with the creation of other living creatures and that he is not a descendent of any lower species of the animal kingdom.)

Many thousands of years later, according to Cerve, a series of magnetic waves began to move around the earth's circuit from east to west, and this affected the then-civilization to such an extent that the Lemurians kept records of the changes. According to this amazing book, the part of the continent of Lemuria that was con-nected with Asia and Africa began to sink, leaving parts of Lemuria submerged. The same magnetic waves, according to the author, affected the continent of what is now Europe and it rose higher. The continents which were destined to became North America and South America began to drift away and separate. As the continent of what is now North America moved westward, it joined with the eastern mountainous coast of Lemuria, and later on, when Lemuria was almost fully submerged, this high eastern terrain of Lemuria (which included Mt. Shasta) joined the western portion of what now constitutes western North America. This would include the states of Washington, Oregon, all of California, a small part of Nevada and parts of Arizona, and Mexico.

Farfetched? Wishar S. Cerve didn't think so. He further theorized that the Lemurians, knowing that the bulk of their vast continent was sinking, moved to parts of what is now Asia, Australia, South America, and of course, the area that still remained of their own continent. He claims that the pure-blooded Lemurians existing today have chosen to remain in an area with climate as near like that of Lemuria as possible, which accounts for their presence in Mt. Shasta.

Quoting Cerve, "Perhaps the most interesting explanations of what was to be found in this locality is that it was not only the ancient seat of hundreds of Lemurians who lived there and manufactured and grew all of the principal necessities and kept them-selves isolated, as did the other group of Lemurians who lived at Santa Barbara many years ago, but that their village itself was only partly on the outside of Mt. Shasta, that there is a tunnel through its eastern base leading to a great enclosure in which there is a city of strange homes, and that the heat and smoke seen arising from the crater of Mt. Shasta was smoke and heat from the interior village."

The Lemurians had schools and physicians, their homes were large and airy, they cooked their food by fire or by the heat of the sun in special sun ovens. They had community swimming pools and bathing pavilions — both sexes bathed at the same time because nudity, as such, meant nothing to them.

There was, according to Cerve, no attempt to seek a long life. They themselves decided when they would die and they were not afraid of death because they believed in reincarnation. It was common for them to announce to their relatives that two or three days hence they would pass through transition, and on that day he (or she) would place himself on a portion of sacred soil which he had selected to be his burial site, close his eyes, and go into eternal sleep within a few hours. The body, after transition, was considered to be of little importance, and the earthly remains were covered with a mineral much like lime which destroyed every vestige of it without contaminating the soil.

The Lemurians reportedly harnessed all of nature's forces and were able to propel their boats in water by using the energy that radiated from a single stone, and they had airships which utilized the same energy.

Cerve stated, "The Lemurians, either by force of circumstances or through a greater understanding of cosmic energies, were able to use the power in many minerals and apply this power very specifically and efficiently. One of the outstanding features of Lemurian scientific achievements was the utilizing of the energy and power that is constantly bathing this earth in sunlight. In our present-day period of scientific achievement, we are just speculating upon this possibility and a few small engines have been constructed which operate with sun power. The Lemurians used this sun power very freely and universally in all of their communities. It gave them light and heat and energy at night, and gave them enormous motive power during the day for the movement of great pieces of stone and wood in their constructive operations."

Also, using their boats and airships, the Lemurians reportedly had a colonization program in which they made pilgrimages to other lands; some reached Africa in their westerly journeys and settled along the shores of the Nile River, and this, according to the author, was the beginning of the Egyptian civilization. He stated that Lemurians settled in and around the rivers and great seas in what is now known as Texas, and also parts of Mexico and Yucatan. These settlers were known under the general name of Mayas, which he said was a general term given to all the Lemurians and even to some of the Atlanteans who had entered that area and built temples and large cities.

If you look at a map of the Gulf of Mexico, you'll see, jutting up into the middle of it from the southern side, a huge peninsula. This is the peninsula of Yucatan and part of Mexico, Today it is a poor, and for the most part, uninhabited country. But at one time it was the home of the Mayas who were known to have had an advanced culture. They built magnificent pyramidal temples, one over 200 feet high and built for some reason over two smaller pyramids. The Maya capital was Chichen Itza. Suddenly, one day, Chichen Itza was abandoned; no one knows why the Mayans left. The entire population, over 100,000, just disappeared, leaving behind their cooking pots on the hearths and their plows in the fields. By the year 1900 the palaces were piles of jumbled stones and the central pyramid merely a grass-covered mound in the forest. The overturned stones, however, were still unbroken so that archeologists were able to clear away the jungle growth and reconstruct the most important buildings. Today the temples and monuments and palaces stand, to a great extent, as they originally were and are an astonishing sight. Many think that these refugees were Lemurians and Atlanteans fleeing again from another catastrophe.

According to Cerve's beliefs, the great cataclysm of fifteen thousand years ago which caused the western portion of the flourishing continent of Atlantis to sink also caused the submersion and destruction of almost all of the civilization as it was known in that part of the world. And then, twelve thousand years ago, in another terrible upheaval the remainder of Atlantis sank, Lemuria was devastated, and her great civilization submerged and lost. All that was left were her colonies throughout the world.

Though the existence of such a colony of Lemurians in Mt. Shasta is discredited by some, there are others who claim to have seen strange lights on the mountain at night, and as the sun sets on the pink-tinged snow, golden temple-like domes have been spotted by others.

Though I have lived in the area for many years, I have never seen a Lemurian. However, I would know one immediately should I ever be so fortunate: tall, graceful, with long flowing hair, clad in long white robes and sandals. Their obvious difference, besides their height, would in be in their facial characteristics because they are said to possess an extra organ in the center of their extra-large foreheads. This walnut-sized protrusion, believed to be a normal organ of the ancient human's general equipment and regarded as a sort of sixth sense, was equivalent to an eye, or nose, and enabled them to communicate among themselves by a sort of telepathy or, as we call it now, extrasensory perception. This organ, it is said, has diminished in size and use down through the ages through general lack of use and is, apparently, almost non-existent today. The Lemurians, according to Cerve, have long, slender necks which they like to adorn with beautiful decorative collars made of precious stones and hair which they braided or arranged in intricate fashion across the shoulders or down the back.

After Cerve's book came out, it should be noted, Lemurians were reportedly seen on the roads on Mt. Shasta. Believers thought that since the Lemurians were wholly undesirous of public attention, they could disappear suddenly, at will. And did. Stories circulated around the village of Mount Shasta that they traded in stores and paid for their purchases with gold nuggets, refusing to accept the change, indicating that to them the gold was of no value and that they had no actual need for money of any kind.

Nowadays such stories have ceased. But the world-wide interest incurred by Cerve's book in 1931 has never subsided. Visitors to the area surrounding Mt. Shasta still ask many questions about the mountain and the Lemurians, and they ask if there is really a colony of them existing deep into the interior of Mt. Shasta, with living quarters containing vast apartments.

photo by Kim McEuen

Chapter 3

Dugja, Queen Of The Lemurians

Mt. Shasta

on a brisk fall morning

engulfed in beautiful

lenticular cloud formations.

Over the years I have interviewed many people on many subjects, even those who claim to have out-of-body visits to Mt. Shasta. Many religions have centered on out-of-body, transcendental experiences. Hindu and Tibetan monks spend their lives perfecting the technique of escaping their bodies — astral travel — but it is much less common in the Judeo-Christian tradition.

The following interview took place in the mid-1970s. A spokesman for a group who call themselves "Elan Vital" phoned and said the group would like to talk to me about a happening on the mountain. Would I be interested?

I invited the group to my home that evening, and they told me they come every year from different parts of the United States to camp near Sand Flat on Mt. Shasta. They explained that Elan Vital means "Vital Essence" which equates to the vital motivating essence that causes everything to be and their purpose was to do positive things to the world.

"Usually about 40 of us come to Mt. Shasta during the summer," said their spokesman, "though our group numbers in the hundreds and we hail from cities all over the United States. Cities which include Tampa, Houston, Chicago, Austin, New York, Eureka, and Los Angeles," said one of the girls.

Then they told me that they meditate, study, commune with nature on the mountain, and some of them talk to Dugja (pronounced Doo-ja) who is a being and reigns supreme as the "Spirit of the Mountain". Dugja, according to the group, can materialize at will and is thought to be the last queen of Lemuria. The legendary Lemurians of Mt. Shasta, they said, were her court.

The leader of the group claimed he knew Dugja in another embodiment on the continent of Lemuria which, he said, flourished between 80,000 B.C. and 150,000 B.C. He said he came to Mt. Shasta for the first time in 1963 after having studied and meditated under several gurus for many years. That same year he became a group leader in Eureka, where he still lived at the time of the interview.

"It took me 18 years to make the progression that it takes my students just four months to make now," he said.

That year, in 1963, he said he hiked up to Grey Butte on Mt. Shasta and paused briefly to meditate. He claims an astral man appeared with thin hair, white beard, and pink skin. The man was wearing a chain-like belt.

He continued his meditation, but he said he felt powerful pressure from the astral man and what seemed like other invisible forces willing him to turn back. He said he felt as though they were forcing him to go back down the mountain.

16

But instead of turning back, he continued up the trail and it was then that he first saw Dugja, who asked him to stay.

Three years later he returned, encountered the same astral man but continued on up the trail. Dugja appeared again and gently said, "Welcome home."

"From that time," he said, "I have returned many times to Mt. Shasta, both physically and astrally."

"Why?" I asked.

"I teach a group there every summer, and I am also responsible for cleaning negative light forces around Mt. Shasta and elsewhere in the world," he replied. "These light forces affect the population and in order to make the world a better place in which to live, I polarize their negative influences. Eventually they will all be pure. In the meantime, I make many astral trips to Mt. Shasta in order to purify the lights."

"Do you always make physical trips during the summer?" I asked.

"Yes." he said. And then he looked fondly at the group. "I come to greet and teach my flock on the sylvan slopes of Mt. Shasta, where the very air and atmosphere is charged with goodness, harmony, and peace."

photo by Sally Abbe

Chapter 4

A Wondrous Strange Happening

There are those

who believe spaceships hide

in the lenticular clouds

that form over Mt. Shasta.

The photo shows a

particularly beautiful cloud

hovering over the

slopes of the mountain.

In the fall of 1979 I received a telephone call from a lady I didn't know. She said she had a story to tell and would I like to hear it? I asked what kind of story and she said the story was about Lemurians. I asked if I could bring a tape recorder and she said yes. The following then, in her exact words, is an account of her startling story:

"It was the first of January, 1976. The television was on but I wasn't really watching it. I was tired because I had been out the night before, it had been New Year's Eve. I was trying to watch the program but I really didn't care much about it.

"My memories of this 'happening' was that I felt, suddenly, an interruption. Then I felt it again. It was getting on towards dusk. Pretty soon I could see vapors — I could see them forming out of the corner of my left eye. I thought to myself 'okay, I know all about this' because for many years I have dealt with exorcism and I have dealt with entities approaching. I can read them and see them. But I wasn't sure what was happening here. I tried to make it out. I was supercognizant that something was happening.

"The movement seemed to be coming from the window, but at that time I didn't realize it. Finally, after a while, after nothing seemed to materialize before me or to confront me (I have experienced these things before), I turned my head and I could see, coming from the top and bottom of the door, this vapor-like substance seeping inside. I was totally mesmerized. I just sat there and... well... just looked. I didn't know what to do. I had never experienced anything like this before. The door was closed and the window was closed and the vapor just came into the room, forward and forward and forward. And then it started to take form.

"A friend of mine was sitting in that wicker chair reading a book. I finally said to her, 'Look'

"The vapors were moving in and taking shape and I realized that I was seeing something unusual that I had never seen before. My friend looked up from her book and then she looked at me. I can't relate to what she saw, but I can relate to how she reacted. She immediately closed the book, sat back, and watched. This went on for about 15 minutes, and all these vapors came in and took form.

"The first form, about eight feet tall, had really high lighting. I can't give you a color, it was just a sensation. There were four more beings that stood behind the first one who were about seven feet tall. Their faces were super-elongated and you couldn't see a mouth. They had on long robes. You couldn't really see any personality, but they were definitely forms standing there in my kitchen for a long while. And we watched them.

"I asked my friend, 'What do you see?' I wanted her to tell me in words what she saw.

'I see all these beings standing there in the kitchen,' she said.

"And the beings just stood there. We kept watching them. The initial being, he was taller. I say 'he' but I don't know that there was he or she in any of them. It just seems that you catch on a gender, but you don't know for sure. Maybe I sensed the being was 'he' because of the power of the vibratory experience, I don't know. Anyway, he disappeared. He left. He just was not there anymore. He left the four other beings, however.

"They continued to stand there and they were emanating a lot of small light vibrations. I can't really explain it. It was like light charging from their beings. Finally, I called my daughter. She had been in her bedroom reading. She came out into the hall, peeked around the corner, and then she looked at me. Her eyes got bigger and she kind of whispered, 'Who are they?' And then I knew that I knew what I was seeing. If both my friend and my daughter were seeing them, too, then it had to be. Because I was still testing. But if they could see these things, too, then it had to be. The beings weren't filmy. We could not see through them. These beings were pulsating. I never saw their hands or anything. Very high conical foreheads. Their eyes I could see, but the rest I could not. But still, at that time, I didn't know where they had come from — my mind was not working at the time. I was not afraid because I have dealt with this sort of thing for a very long time, on many different levels. Reincarnated beings that are earthbound.

"My daughter came in and sat down, and my friend came over and sat on the couch with me. The beings were staying there. So I tried putting some questions out to them and I got the answers. I started to tell the girls, and then I thought 'they're not going to believe what I'm saying.' You know? I sensed this. So my friend said she had a ouija board that she had never used, not ever.

"I didn't know about that, Ouija boards are not one of my things. But she brought it out and in the next hour and a half we asked them questions. Many, many, many questions. We asked the beings about my daughter, my friend, and myself, and everything that was told to us happened in the length of time that we were questioning them. That I can tell you. That I know...

"We asked them where they were from and they said they were from the mountain. That they were originally from Lemuria. We asked about the saucers. They replied that the saucers were here to re-seed the planet. We were told that when the devastation comes, they will re-seed the planet.

"We asked if saucers really land here and they said 'yes' and then they made it plain to us that they wanted to talk to my daughter. Their sole purpose in coming here was to talk to her. They wanted her to do certain things that she 'knew about' from her relationship with them a long time ago. They told her that she was a former Lemurian. They called her their high priestess.

"None of us knew anything about this and my daughter was really upset. She kept closing off the whole thing. Further and further. And they told her other things, very private things. But she was acting as though she didn't believe any of this was going on, as though she didn't want to believe it. As though she didn't want to know what was happening. And she has been very careful about talking about it ever since.

"By this time we were communicating through mental telepathy, too. And they gave her a time and they gave her a limit, seven months. And within that time, certain happenings that they told her about actually happened. What they wanted her to do was a really detailed thing, and they did not reveal it to me nor to my friend. My daughter understood and she knew. So, she started questioning them. She had made tentative plans to move to Washington, and she asked if she could do this thing if she moved from Mount Shasta.

"And then they were gone. I mean, those beings who had been here for an hour and a half, were gone. My daughter got up from her chair, ran across the kitchen, out the backdoor, and looked up to the mountain. She was crying. But they had told her that there would be one of them with her at all times — it might not necessarily be the same one — until she made up her mind what she was going to do. In other words, would she do as they asked, or not?

"Now I know what it is they wanted her to do, but it is not mine to tell. It was given to me to know. It has something to do with her connection with them. And she did not do it. It was not a simple thing to do, it had something to do with the mountain. About long-ago, very old information that they were trying to bring up. That's as much as I can tell you except that it involved people living in the city of Mount Shasta.

"But they said, that night, that they do exist inside the mountain in another form. They live in another realm. During the time they were here, we lit a candle when it got dark and there was a blue glow all over the kitchen. We were told there is a whole city within Mt. Shasta but that they live in a different realm. The beings told my daughter to stay here, do what they asked, and they would help her; but she didn't do as they asked. They said it was time to reveal certain information from long ago, that it was time to make people aware of what's going on here, right now. They gave her the possible accessibility to these facts. But what can I say. She couldn't accept the responsibility. She was too young.

"They were 'here' for about six weeks after that. There was a hum and a vibration in this house you wouldn't believe. It was beautiful, you could hear it. And there were certain incidents that happened that made you aware that they were here. After that night we decided that we would try to contact them and it was immediate. We got the same rapport. The energy was still there. But when, finally, my daughter decided not to make a commitment, then it wasn't here anymore. It has been gone for a long time.

"My daughter has a thing to learn, but she'll be back. As for me, I'm a suspicious person, but I know the things that happened that night. It sounds crazy and I know that. Do what you want with it. But it happened."

After the interview that autumn evening, I asked the lady — who wishes to remain anonymous — to sign a release on her strange story, which she did. I have kept the story in my files, waiting to find out if the daughter ever made the commitment. It is now over ten years later, and I'm still waiting.

photo courtesy of the Mansfield family

Chapter 5

Abraham Mansfield
and the
Plates of Time

Abraham Mansfield

believed that Lemurian gold mines

exist deep within Mt. Shasta

and wrote several books about

mines and other phenomena.

He claimed that he was

the appointed

Chief of the Gods of the Lemurians.

As you undoubtedly know by now, mystery and intrigue are synonymous with Mt. Shasta. Therefore, throughout the years I've met fascinating people with stories to tell. Abraham Mansfield was one of them. For years, until his death, we were in touch, we also corresponded and enjoyed long sessions on the telephone in which he would regale me with wonderful (and bizarre) stories concerning his life as Chief of the Gods of the Lemurians.

Mansfield was a colorful character and I liked him. He had been around, a lot, and he'd had many fascinating experiences. Then he began recording them in books. The following is from his book entitled, *The Golden Goddess of the Lemurians* and he gave me permission to quote from it. But first, let me set the scene:

The year was 1931. Mansfield tells of the experiences of his friend (not named in the book for personal reasons) who had lost his way on the northeast side of Mt. Shasta while following a wounded deer. He finally found the dead buck, but he had become completely lost and had wandered around until he was exhausted. Quoting from Mansfield's book, "About 3:30 a.m. he heard someone saying, 'Why don't you come with me?' My friend looked up and to his surprise there stood a being seven feet tall who said, 'I am a Lemurian. What are you doing here?'"

The author then divulges the experiences of his friend, who was taken voluntarily to a palace and gardens beneath Mt. Shasta. His friend and the Lemurian kept going down, down, down and finally the Lemurian said, "We are here in the shaft of gold and it is only a little farther to my cave, which is lined with gold. You can sleep on my slab of gold. You will not need blankets because the slab was heated chemically thousands of years ago and never loses its constant heat. It is similar to the sun."

The golden pillow was placed under the man's head and he was told, "Think of what time you would prefer to awaken and you will, as the pillow is a mental-thought pillow, radiated, so you will become acquainted with mental seance, like the other Lemurians of the living-dead beings."

The man was also told, according to Mansfield, that there were a series of tunnels and shafts, or flues, left by the volcanoes which were connected together under the earth like highways — like a world within a world — and the shafts went several hundred miles in any direction. As for the brightness in that underworld, he was told that the walls were painted with a liquid sunshine and were as bright in all the caverns as though the sun itself were shining through.

One shaft, he was told, led to the ocean and was near the wilds of Del Norte County, 90 miles to the west, near a monastery that was built to train religious Lemurians, and that this shaft, lined with gold, was accessible from the outside.

"I saw," the man told Mansfield later, "plates and gold-lined shafts, and tables and chairs unbelievably monstrous in size. Then I asked the Lemurian about the beings. He said they had gone to the center of the earth, to a far better world than that which existed near the surface in the volcanic caverns, and that he would take me there if I wished."

The bewildered man, however, decided to return to the surface, mostly to see if he were, indeed, still alive. The Lemurian agreed to take him back, explaining that he could not be taken to the surface until he was decongested, explaining that otherwise he would die upon entering the surface when confronting the outside air.

After thinking it over, the man decided to stay and see a few more sights before returning. He told Mansfield later, "I wanted to see the Lemurian treasure vaults and things from the long-ago Etruscian and Lemurian civilizations. The Lemurian said the crown jewels and gold were there, but there was nothing about their way of life as they never kept scientific records at the mines. The gold was taken out for all nations of the world and they built temples with gold on the islands of Etrucia and Lemuria." The Lemurian, according to Mansfield's book, told the man that he grew carrots 2 feet long and 2 feet through, and all other vegetables and fruits the same. He showed the crown jewels of the Lemurian and Etrucian civilizations of thousands of years ago and said the Lemurian and Etrucian treasure vaults are still there, the way they were left after the Ice Age. And that it had been quite a feat to force the water out and reseal the tunnels and caves, which he said had been done thousands of years ago. He was told the survivors of Lemuria found these flues, and also that they had brought their reactors from their homeland on the island which sank into the ocean from high tides and earthquakes in the receding of the last Ice Age. (Quoting Mansfield from his book: "Before the Ice Age, the ocean was five miles from what is now Mt. Shasta.")

Finally, after seeing other wonders, the man asked to be returned to the surface.

"I told the Lemurian," he told Mansfield later, "that I would like to return to see if I was still actually alive, and find my car and my friend who had been hunting with me when I got lost. I explained that he must be worried by now as I had my car keys in my pocket and it was a long walk home for him."

Thereupon, he was decongested and returned safely to the surface.

He told Mansfield after they were reunited, "On the outside he left me on my own again and completely disappeared into the depths of the mountain. I wandered around looking for the road and my car. Finally I said to myself 'you fool, get down off this mountain and start over. Go up the Old Emigrant Road that you were on and find your car where you and Mansfield left it yesterday or whatever day it was.'"

He found his car and Mansfield, who said he had nearly frozen to death the night before. As they left the mountain they compared notes, discovering they had both had former eerie experiences, and Mansfield revealed that he was acquainted with the shafts of gold and the Plates of Time from happenings in his own life. His friend said to him, "You speak of the shaft lined with gold, the Plates of Time, and the Eucheon of God's sciences. I saw the Eucheon on the walls of the cave I slept in. And as the Plates of Time state, it is time to tell the world, and you were the one chosen for the mission."

In a separate letter to Mansfield, I asked about the Plates of Time and the reason for their existence.

"The Plates of Time," he explained, "were assembled thousands of years ago. The Ice Age was coming on, which meant total destruction. The rulers of that ancient civilization were highly educated and had highly civilized sciences including atomic power. They tried to combat the ice flows by melting them. They blew deep holes in the earth; the more melting, the more water, earthquakes, and volcanic action. Their civilization was destroyed by the use of atomic power.

"The Plates of Time were assembled for future generations to preserve the knowledge they had about atomic power so that a new generation would use it wisely and respect the powers of God, and any and all things from beginning to end, of all worlds and time."

Abraham Joseph Mansfield shown wearing coronation garb that he wore in 1934 when he reputedly was appointed Chief of the Gods of the Lemurians.

photo by Neil & Carl Clement

Chapter 6

Queen Etruceana

Business men,

residents and ranchers,

all spoke freely of the

Lemurians and their community.

Some told of rituals

at sunset, midnight,

and dawn.

*I*ndeed, the late Abraham Mansfield had a story to tell. He believed that Lemurians flourished in the Mt. Shasta area and he wrote a book in which he revealed the secrets of the Lemurian gold mines and also the circumstances which led to his unexpected appointment and coronation as Chief of the Gods of the Lemurians, an honor which enabled him to view what he called the Plates of Time which deal with mathematical equations and dimensions of secret solar control of atomic energy. He also received one-sixth of Queen Etruceana's jewels.

Queen Etruceana? Who was she, and how does she fit into this story? Well, I will endeavor to explain it to you as Mansfield explained it to me.

I was writing for the *Dunsmuir News*, a small weekly newspaper in extreme northern California, when his book, *The Golden Goddess of the Lemurians* came out in 1970, and he sent me a copy. He also sent enough strange material on Mt. Shasta to fill four large manila envelopes. Some of it was confusing to me, but he swore it was all true.

Mansfield said the Plates of Time are the treasured and ancient Sciences of God from the very beginning and relate to a people deceased thousands of years ago. They dwelled on a chain of islands which sank into the oceans which we know now as the Atlantic Ocean and the Pacific Ocean; they were islands which included Etrucia, Lemuria, Atlantis, and Oceantis.

According to Mansfield, these prehistoric civilizations had far greater knowledge than we do of atom power, ESP, electronics, and science, and could pick up messages that were recorded in time and space from back civilizations to the beginning of time. He said the Etrucian-Lemurian story and the Plates of Time have been around for thousands of years, and his theory was as follows:

Down the dim corridors of the ages, the world was different than it is now and many islands flourished which have since sank to the bottom of the oceans. Among them were the above mentioned islands, and they were ruled by Queen Etruceana, as was the entire world as it was known then, through a Ten Nations Council. Her husband, the king, was interested in other things. He was a great scientist and spent much of his time viewing foreign planets, building pyramids, and great towers.

It appears, however, that the king was sterile. Queen Etruceana wanted sons to rule the world so she took the ten kings of the Ten Nation Council, one at a time, and produced six sons and one daughter. Thus endowed with future kings, she and her sons would continue to rule the world. Her plan was interrupted, however, when the Ice Age started. Mansfield claims in his book that the world tipped from north to south, throwing the South Pole of the equator on the opposite side of the earth. In the chain of events, he wrote, all the ocean currents were forced to flow northward.

Quoting Mansfield, "It was like a giant trough around the center of the earth, with a rim on both sides and the middle."

Knowing of the impending disaster, Queen Etruceana and her king ordered ten million Etrucians and Mongols to build reed boats with a light wooden structure. These boats were designed to hold 10,000 people and enough food to last until they could get to the top of the ice floe and recede with it.

Then, when the expected second tip of the world came, all that could boarded the boats and headed north. It was natural for them to go north, according to Mansfield, north was safest because the safest place at the time of the Ice Age was at the top of the ice floe. Some took refuge on the highest parts of what is now South America (at one time Etrucia), some took refuge on any high land which protruded above the water.

At the time of the disaster, Queen Etruceana decreed that her six son-kings would be kings forever in heredity, even from the world beyond. The survivors of the Ice Age diligently kept track of the descendants of these sons through mental seances in order to find the rightful heirs to rule as the Chief of the Gods of the Lemurians, a reign, said Mansfield, that changes every thirty years, even now.

Also decreed was that the Inca nation was to train their chiefs, find the rightful king in heredity, and entrust to them the scientific knowledge of the Plates of Time so as to keep the knowledge on the plates forever alive. Or to quote Mansfield, "Until our present civilization should become as enlightened in sciences as were those who lived then."

The manner in which Abraham Joseph Mansfield became Chief of the Gods of the Lemurians was, as he said, through mental seance. He wrote, "I haven't any idea just how James Churchward, who served the reign from 1874 to 1904, figured out the original Etrucian scriptures, or how Arthur J. Cowdray (who also appears in this book as J. C. Brown) from 1904 to 1934, figured out the Plates of Time unless Queen Etruceana, the mother of the English language, had them revised into English. But Arthur Cowdray figured out the Eucheon. Mansfield thought Cowdray figured it out in his mine in the Sierras, during the long winters, and had written a book about it but burned it — he said he didn't want to be called a fool again as he claimed he was during 1904 and 1934 with regards to the Lemurian treasure he saw and the Plates of Time."

And so it was, in a bizarre chain of events, that Mansfield became Chief of the Gods of the Lemurians in 1934, in a ceremony performed at sunrise in the wilds of Del Norte County, at the "throne" which was situated east of the Lemurian monastery under the cliffs at the heads of Bluff and Blue Creeks near Cinder Cone Peak. In that ceremony, Mansfield claims the honor entitled him to one-sixth of Queen Etruceana's jewels, and also ownership to a most valuable Lemurian gold mine within the deep recesses of Mt. Shasta, a shaft in which gold hung like icicles.

Mansfield states in his book that he was a member of the American Institute of Electrical and Electronic Engineers, and that he was born with a highly sensitized scientific and photographic mind. He claims to have also been blessed with the powers of extrasensory perception. He said he fully understood the equations and dimensions of atomic energy, the secret of which he was privileged to view on the prehistoric Plates of Time at his coronation. This privilege, he said, was handed down to him through heredity from the ancient and enlightened Etrucean, Lemurian, and Atlantean civilizations. His reign ended in 1964, after 30 years, and he decided to write about it.

What's more, he had Queen Etruceana's jewels to prove it. One was a bracelet with "Etruceana" engraved inside. The ornate bracelet is designed with ten major crowns and 26 lesser crowns which represented the large and small nations of the world as it was when she reigned. He said Queen Etruceana wore this bracelet at all the meetings of the Ten Nation Council which were held on the island of Etrucia, at the time the largest of the islands. Also included was a set of royal platinum serving ware embossed with angels, plus the queen's coronation bracelet, a pendant, other jewelry and an actual faded likeness of prehistoric Queen Etruceana.

When Abraham Mansfield passed on several years ago, I felt that certainly he was one of the most colorful and interesting of all the people I've ever interviewed. And other stories have appeared unexpectedly which seems to corroborate his story. For instance, he told of a news story involving an Inca princess. Her name was Xegmoo Winomoo, who was found by natives frozen in the ice of the northern part of the world above Labrador.

She was, Mansfield wrote, clad in Inca princess garb, with a bracelet on each arm and necklaces around her neck. One of the hand-made golden chains was six feet long with a jeweled memory powder-bucket attached. Naturally, questions arose as to how she had gotten there, and according to Mansfield, newspapers and magazines published the curious event. (Nearby in the ice was found a frozen dinosaur, still fresh, which the natives found to be edible.)

The natives notified Russian and Norwegian governments, who, in turn, notified the Inca nation, which Mansfield said was located east of the Amazon and east of the Andes and reportedly inhabited by descendants of original Etrucian-Mongol natives. Whereupon an Inca medicine man boarded a ship to the Lace Islands, found, and buried the princess, and then brought back her jewelry and identification so that it might be recorded as belonging to the Etrucian-Lemurian civilizations on the Plates of Time.

Princess Xegmoo Winomoo, it seems, was a descendant of Queen Etruceana and this was verified by a curious fact: When the islands began to sink, Queen Etruceana cut the brail (rope) of her crown and gave her king-sons and her daughter each a piece of it, so that they could be easily recognized as royalty if lost or found dead in the flight for survival. When the princess was found, she had one of the pieces of brail embedded in the top of a lotus blossom bracelet which she was wearing on her fatal flight north.

Mansfield said the princess was found frozen in fresh water, not ocean water, so it was assumed that she had gotten off the boat somewhere on the journey, obviously could not survive, and was frozen apparently as she was making a step because she was found in an upright position and standing in a slight stoop-position.

Mansfield had her bracelet, too, in his possession along with Queen Etruceana's ornate jewelry and platinum serving ware. Also presented to him at the time of his coronation was an ancient dynasty chest, an ornately-carved treasure chest, a drum, an enormous chair, and, strangely enough, the jewelry of James Fairchild, otherwise known as James Churchward, author of *The Lost Continent of Mu,* and the jewelry of the elusive Lord Aurthur J. Cowdray, also known as J. C. Brown.

J. C. Brown weaves an intricate pattern through Mansfield's remarkable book, always mysterious, always involved with the enigma of those same prehistoric islanders of that lost age who reportedly journeyed regularly from their islands to Mt. Shasta. The ocean at that time was within five miles of the base of Mt. Shasta, according to the author, the mountain contained enormous underground gold mines which extended several hundred miles.

Oddly enough, this same J. C. Brown Mansfield writes about figures heavily in another book I discovered years ago. It's a book which seems to substantiate Mansfield's theories about the very baffling J. C. Brown. The book entitled *Lost Mines and Hidden Treasure* was written by Leland Lovelace, published by the Naylor Company. Lovelace wrote that J. C. Brown spent the last thirty years of his life trying to unlock the Lemurian mysteries after having had a private and spectacular view of the Lemurian treasure caverns.

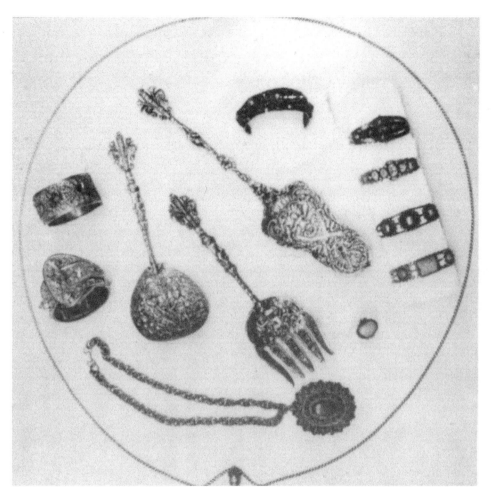

The above photo shows Queen Etruceana's jewelry and her royal platinum serving spoons and fork, which are embossed with angels. Her ornate bracelet, made of ocean water chloride-of-gold (which Mansfield says is extremely light because the ocean atoms of gold are hollow in the minutest forms) has "Etruceana" engraved inside.

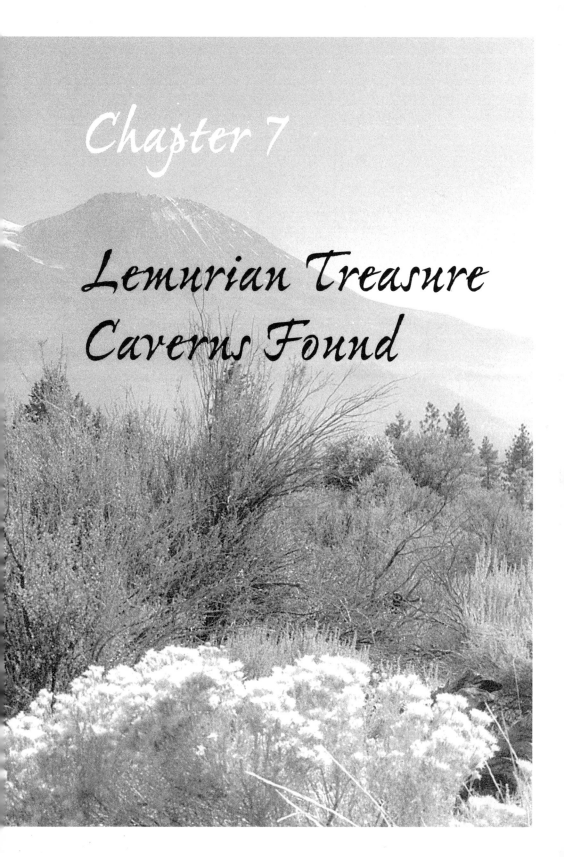

Chapter 7

Lemurian Treasure Caverns Found

He came upon a

macabre scene:

in one chamber he counted

27 skeletons, the

smallest

of which

was 6'6" and the

largest

stretching out to

more than 10 feet.

*I*t would be well to remember that Abraham Mansfield was well acquainted with J. C. Brown, whom he said was actually Lord Arthur J. Cowdray operating under an alias.

According to author Leland Lovelace in his book *Lost Mines and Hidden Treasure* the Lord Cowdray Mining Company of London, England, hired J. C. Brown to prospect some gold properties for them in 1904 in the northern mountains of California. (I also read this story in a 1967 issue of *Western Treasures* magazine.)

While at Mt. Shasta, in northern California, he ran onto a section of rock in the face of a cliff which didn't seem to match the surrounding formation. While examining the curious stone, he noticed it blocked the entrance to what appeared to be a cave. Brown, a geologist, thought the entire scene was unnatural and began to dig out the mouth of the cave which was full of debris and vegetation. He could see that it was not a small cave and after much digging found himself in a tunnel which curved downward into the mountain.

Equipped with lanterns and miner's paraphernalia, he set out to explore. Three miles from the mouth of the tunnel he struck a cross-section containing gold-bearing ore, and farther on he struck another cross-section where an ancient race had apparently mined copper.

He believed the other cross-sections outcropped on some other part of the mountain. The decline continued, and about eleven miles inside the mountain he found what he called "the village." He discovered two rooms filled with copper and gold tablets, about three by four inches and concave, laid one inside the other. The rooms were literally full of these plates, all inscribed neatly.

The walls, he said later, were lined with tempered copper and hung with shields and wall-pieces made of gold. On some of the golden plates he found were engraved certain drawings and hieroglyphics. There were tempered copper spears and other objects made of gold. Rooms opened into other chambers, one of which appeared to have been a place of worship: there were 13 statues made of copper and gold and a large sun design from which protruded golden streamers.

Because of the way the objects were strewn about, he had the feeling the occupants of the underground village had left on the spur of the moment. And then he came upon a macabre scene: in one chamber he counted 27 skeletons, the smallest of which was 6'6" and the largest stretching out more than 10 feet. Two of the bodies were mummified, each clad in colorful, ornate robes.

Brown spent days exploring, taking notes, studying the hieroglyphics and indelibly imprinting them in his mind. He was excited about this great archeological find but decided to leave the tunnel and its contents exactly as he had found them. He would return. But first he cleverly concealed the entrance of the tunnel and marked on his map exactly where it was.

The next three decades, those spanning 1904-1934, Brown's activities seem to be shrouded in mystery but it is known that he studied the literature and philosophy pertaining to the lost continent of Lemuria (Mu) and the lost Lemurian civilization among other lore of prehistoric races. Years of study and comparison of the hieroglyphics and pictographs he had found in the tunnel convinced him that they were, indeed, records of the Lemurian race.

And so, after 30 long years, Brown surfaced. He decided that the golden artifacts still hanging untouched in the cavern and the glory of those Lemurians should be shared by others.

His age probably had something to do with this magnanimous decision because at the age of 79 he appeared in Stockton, California. The year was 1934. His idea was to organize a group of people interested in accompanying him, at his expense, to Mt. Shasta, and once there they would explore further the ancient tunnel he had discovered in 1904.

Eighty eager Stockton residents including a newspaper editor, a museum curator, a retired printer, several scientists, and other solid citizens formed a group to investigate the tunnel with J. C. Brown. They met nightly for six weeks to plan the expedition and also to listen to Brown's fabulous tales of lost continents, hieroglyphics, and the enticing descriptions of the treasure which seemed to be just within their grasp. Some even gave up their jobs and sold much of their personal property during those six weeks, so certain were they that their lives would be altered and enriched after their remarkable discoveries.

The editor and the curator questioned Brown closely, going over and over the details of his bizarre story. Brown disclosed that he had spent much of the previous 30 years searching for ancient records pertaining to the Lemurians, and his mental pictures of the hieroglyphics in the tunnel village had convinced him that he had found the lost link in the story of civilization.

He told them, and the group, that he believed the golden antiquities he had found in the cavernous rooms inside Mt. Shasta were those of the Lemurians or their descendants.

Brown even promised to provide a yacht to transport the group as far north as they could go by water. They would leave on June 19th at 1:00 p.m.

The day dawned clear and beautiful and 80 Stockton citizens were waiting at the designated time for their leader to appear. They had met the evening before in order to consummate the final details, after which J. C. Brown bid them adieu until the next afternoon.

J. C. Brown, however, was never seen by the Stockton group again and what happened to him is anybody's guess. The members of the group feared for his life: he had mentioned that he had once been kidnapped and had barely escaped with his life.

They called in the Stockton police but no trace of the man was found. He had completely disappeared. Had he changed his mind?

The members of the group were completely bewildered, but they still believed the authenticity of his story, and they still believed in the existence of the vast tunnel in Mt. Shasta filled with Lemurian treasures.

Unfortunately, Brown had never revealed the exact location of the secret tunnel in the mountain. It was in an area so vast that it is highly improbable that those treasures of a prehistoric era will ever again delight the eyes of another human.

There are some interesting coincidences concerning J. C. Brown. Author Leland Lovelace mentions the fact that the career of J. C. Brown, after his discovery of the hidden treasure of the Lemurians in 1904, was shrouded in mystery for the next 30 years.

According to Abraham Mansfield's book, J. C. Brown and Lord Arthur J. Cowdray were one and the same and he was a mining engineer from England who reigned as Chief of the Gods of the Lemurians from 1904–1934, which accounts for that 30-year gap before he allegedly surfaced in Stockton.

All of which leads to pure conjecture. Was J. C. Brown presented with a map to the treasure cavern of the Lemurians after his appointment as Chief of the Gods of the Lemurians in 1904? It is hardly conceivable that he found the cavern accidentally on a mountain as huge as 14,162-foot Mt. Shasta.

We will never know because Brown died in 1936 and is buried, according to a Basque sheepherder, in the Black Desert of Nevada, near the famed Lost Padre Mine.

But he lived on in the memory of Abraham Mansfield because when J. C. Brown's term ended in 1934 as Chief of the Gods of the Lemurians, Mansfield's 30-year reign began and it wasn't until it ended in 1964 that he felt he could tell his story.

And so he told it. Believe it or not...

photo by Neil & Carl Clement

Chapter 8

Atlanteans In Mt. Shasta?

This

shining peak

rises in

solitary splendor

14,162'

into

northern California's

blue sky.

Incredibly, still another booklet came to light in which the author, Dr. M. Doreal, contradicts the legend that the mountain is inhabited by Lemurians. He states in a publication entitled *Mysteries of Mount Shasta* which was published by the Brotherhood of the White Temple, Sedalia, Colorado, that the survivors of Atlantis inhabit the mountain.

Dr. Doreal's theory goes along with the belief that northern California is one of the most ancient lands in the world. But he claims that before the sinking of Lemuria and Atlantis, there already existed an Atlantean colony in northern California and that when Atlantis and Lemuria finally submerged, the survivors of Atlantis fled to the mountains, forming a colony inside Mt. Shasta where they live today, although they have gradually decreased in number. Dr. Doreal claimed there were 353 at the time of his visit to the Atlantean colony in 1931.

As for the Lemurians, Dr. Doreal contends they built their civilization in the South Pacific, the remains of which can be seen in the Caroline Islands. Their temples were placed atop the mountains which existed at that time, and the great basalt walls of the ancient structures still stand.

These Lemurians reportedly built vast subterranean pleasure cities beneath the mountains, and they also attained a scientific and intellectual mastership beyond any modern achievements, harnessing nature's forces and utilizing the energies from the sun and the moon. Using this mastery freely, they were able to heat and light their subterranean cities. They also knew the secret of the atom.

According to Dr. Doreal, however, the Atlanteans and the Lemurians engaged in a great war, after which the Lemurian royalty, priest-kings, and noblemen withdrew in defeat to their underground pleasure palaces where they remain today in captivity. After their retreat, the Atlantean victors sealed the entrance and established an elaborate guard system which prohibits the Lemurians to ever escape their bondage.

The Atlanteans, Dr. Doreal states, still reside in their colony beneath Mt. Shasta and commute every three months by strange cigar-shaped airships to that area in the South Pacific in order to check the sealed entrance of the imprisoned Lemurians (which believers say accounts for the appearance of space ships in the Mt. Shasta area).

An interesting part of the booklet deals with Dr. Doreal's visit, by invitation, to the Atlantean city many miles beneath Mt. Shasta. He explains in detail how the invitation came about and how he was transported from Topanga Canyon in southern California to a place two-thirds up the side of Mt. Shasta, to a building fashioned from rose-colored stone.

From this place he and his companions were transported to the very top of the mountain. Walking over to the center of an enormous flat rock spanning five acres, they sank rapidly into the interior of the mountain through what seemed to be a sliding shaft of rock. After a five-mile descent they reached a huge cavern situated between great pillars of unusual white metal which, he was told, only existed in ancient Atlantis.

Again descending into the depths of Mt. Shasta 7 more miles, they were brought to an enormous underground space extending 20 miles long and over 10 thousand feet high. The entire area was brightly illuminated and the source seemed to emanate from a centered mass of glowing light. Dr. Doreal described the light as having unusual qualities which made his body tingle. It was said to be a concentrated blending of the sun and moon rays.

He was told that from three power houses hidden on the mountain, the Atlanteans periodically draw from the energies of the sun, moon, and cosmic rays. These rays are directed into the mountain to form the great glowing mass of energy which they use in numerous ways.

According to the booklet, he was then taken to a small city about a mile and a half from the elevator which had borne him underground. This city, he wrote, was incredibly beautiful, with breathtaking white houses built of marble and other stone, architecturally so splendid that the most magnificent temples of ancient Greece were rough caricatures by comparison. The entire subterranean area was landscaped with lovely parks, gardens, and trees. Fruit trees bore fruit unlike any grown today. Dr. Doreal said they had preserved the plants, vegetables, and even some of the animals which had flourished on Atlantis thousands of years ago. Furthermore, they controlled different energies which caused the plants to grow perfectly and periodically condensed moisture when it was needed.

Eating, it was explained to Dr. Doreal, was indulged in strictly for pleasure. They actually had no need for food because the same energy which supplied the light also supplied them with, in every vital breath they drew, the energy for existence.

After they had shown how they could make from common earth any stone or metal they needed and after it had been explained that they live approximately 150 years and then pass of their own free will (transition), and finally, after exhibiting their amazing artistry in the design and weaving of clothing, the Atlanteans then escorted Dr. Doreal to the largest building, their temple.

Their temple was primarily a temple of learning, according to Doreal. Occasionally, he was told, the Atlanteans bring in from the outer world certain chosen ones for instructions, and this temple beneath Mt. Shasta is one of the two places on the North American continent that is used by the "Great White Lodge," and it is one of the places where their work is directed to the outside world.

Dr. Doreal concludes his booklet with the belief that these Atlantean survivors are masters of all the laws of nature, and that they work continuously together with chosen ones in the outside world in order to gradually awaken mankind to the awareness of the great mysteries behind matter and substance, indeed, behind life itself.

And so it is ever thus with this bewitching mountain, which seems to beckon not only the ancients but also earthly humanitarians wishing to create a better universe.

photo by Ed Stockton

Chapter 9

Nola Van Valer: Founder of the Radiant School

I had the feeling that

here was a powerful personality

with a mental force as clear as it

had been when Van Valer had

admittedly met Phylos the Tibetan,

and other "Ascended Masters"

on the McCloud side of

Mt. Shasta during the 1930's.

Nola Van Valer admitted me into her living room and after we had exchanged pleasantries I was invited to sit down. She sat beside me in her wheelchair, an attractive, white-haired, bright-blue-eyed lady in her eighties. In spite of fact that she had fallen, broken her hip, and wasn't feeling well, I had the feeling that here was a powerful personality with a mental force as clear as it had been when Van Valer had admittedly met Phylos the Tibetan and other "Ascended Masters" on the McCloud side of Mt. Shasta during the 1930s. It is believed by many that there are converging rays of cosmic power on Mt. Shasta which make it easier for humans to contact beings they call Ascended Masters and it was to this mountain that Van Valer came in 1930, totally unprepared for the unexpected events which were to follow.

She said she came with her husband and friends to camp on Mt. Shasta at Widow Springs. They lived in San Jose where he was a mechanic and where she attended meetings of the Christian Science Church and also practiced healing. It was during the depression, so they brought along a tent, some cooking utensils and found a lovely place to camp beside a meandering stream.

One day, she said, a strange man appeared before them. He was dressed in a long robe, he "looked pure," and he explained that he had been watching them and had many things he wanted to tell them. As there were no tape recorders at that time, she said she took everything they were told in shorthand. Her time on the mountain began in 1930 and continued every year for 10 years. Sometimes she and others stayed a month or longer. Because of what she learned and other happenings on Mt. Shasta, Van Valer later founded the Radiant School of the Seekers and Servers, using her experiences to form the lessons for her school.

Van Valer believed she had found a working truth. Not knowing what the future held, she and others moved to the city of Mount Shasta and in 1963 established the school. They created and sponsored the "Friendly Letter Service" which reached into thirty-four countries throughout the world. The material covered included powers, elements, forces, energies, magnetism, and also interpretations by Phylos the Tibetan concerning spiritual beings, spirit beings, holy spirits, ethereal realms, astral realms, and terrestrial realms. The group, she said, wished to teach Christian philosophy in a clear, truthful and straight-forward manner.

The following is my interview conducted with Nola Van Valer in the winter of 1973, which she later signed for release:

"Why did Phylos the Tibetan and others appear to some and not to others?" I asked.

"The opportunity is at hand," Nola replied. "If it is intended for you to see, you will see whether you believe it or not. We just happened to be in the right place at the right time."

"But why you suppose it happens to some and not to others," I persisted.

"Because some are more suitable for it and perhaps have earned it through their different lives. Some people seem to receive that do not earn it, but they had to have earned it in some way or another or they would not receive."

"Why do you think the Ascended Masters chose to come to this particular mountain during the 1930s?"

"Because that was the season," she replied. "And Mt. Shasta is a magnetic mountain, so much so that some planes cannot fly over it."

"Are you still in contact with any of the Ascended Masters you met in the 1930s?" She smiled. "Oh, absolutely."

"Have you seen St. Germain who reportedly appeared to Guy Ballard on the mountain during that same time?"

"Oh yes, I've seen St. Germain. Mr. Ballard was up on the mountain the same time we were, and what he received, I will verify."

"To your knowledge," I asked, "were there any other people who saw the Ascended Masters during that time?"

"Oh yes. There were other people. I don't know all of them."

"But they didn't do anything about it?"

"No. I didn't either for a while. I was afraid of what the world would think."

Van Valer then explained that she came to Mt. Shasta every year for ten years until the beings no longer appeared on the mountain. During these times she visited a temple inside a cavern, which she said was visible from the highway. She and others visited the temple for 10 years. Inside was Phylos the Tibetan, who, she said, taught the Bible as it was originally written. There were other Ascended Masters in the temple.

"Is the cavern and temple still there?" I asked.

"As far as I know," she said. "I haven't been able to go up on the mountain for years."

"Was Phylos there every time you were there?"

"Oh, absolutely."

"Does that mean he's always there?"

"No," she replied, "he isn't."

"Then where is he when he isn't inside Mt. Shasta?"

"I would say in the heavenly realms." She shook her head slightly and then said, "I wouldn't know otherwise."

I hoped I wasn't tiring her, but I continued the interrogation. "The temple you refer to inside the mountain is reputed to be one of the eighteen sacred temples in the world where Phylos appears. Is this true?"

"As far as I know. And not only Phylos — many Masters were there."

"I read in an interview you gave recently that Jesus was the son of Elohim, is that correct?"

"Yes. Elohim is the Heavenly Father. Elohim is the family name of the God who created man."

"Are you saying that the God who created man is not the Almighty God?"

"He is just one of the Gods," she replied.

"Who is the Almighty God?"

"I couldn't tell you. I never met him."

I had read in yet another interview that Van Valer claimed to have met Jesus on the mountain during those ten years. I had to ask her.

"Yes, I met Jesus. And he doesn't look like the pictures and paintings we've all seen. He's about average height. He doesn't have long hair, nor a beard. He doesn't look anything like we've been led to believe. He's light-complected."

"Do you think he is a powerful being — God?"

"He's the son of the God who created man."

I had to think about that for a moment. "Do you believe that he was born of the Virgin Mary, that he was on this earth?"

"Yes, I do. Every word of the Bible is true."

"And do you believe," I added, "that he was crucified, buried, rose from dead, and ascended into heaven?"

"He ascended," Van Valer said. "The Bible doesn't say he ascended into heaven. That's the trouble. So many people think the Bible says that and it doesn't. They think it the way they want to think it. Jesus ascended."

I pondered that a while. "You were once quoted as saying that a new Messiah is coming?"

"There will not be a new Messiah," Van Valer said softly. "He will come anew. Jesus will come anew. He will be here by the year 2000, maybe before. A great change is taking place over the earth. By the year 2000 we will not be anything like we are now. A great change is coming. True religion will be in existence all over the world."

"What's going to happen then? Will everyone live in peace and harmony?"

"There will be peace. It will be a new world. There is no hell, we make our own discomforts. That's a good name for them."

We sat quietly for a while. "How many belong to your Radiant School?" I finally asked.

"I couldn't tell you. There are students all over the world. I don't have anything to do in connection with the work at the present time. I'm just not able to do it."

"I understand that you took the teachings down in shorthand when you were on the mountain. Is this what you send out to your students, what you were taught on Mt. Shasta?"

"Not altogether. What I was taught, yes, but not word for word."

"What did the Masters say about the Bible?" I asked this remarkable woman.

"Every word in the Bible is true but it has been misinterpreted. I was taught the correct way of interpreting the Bible."

"How often do you meet the Ascended Masters?"

"Whenever they wish to meet," she replied.

"Do you think they still appear on the mountain?"

Nola Van Valer paused a moment. "They don't stay there. They don't have to stay there. In the Bible, all through it, the Ascended Masters appeared. They weren't called 'Ascended Masters'; they were called 'Sacred Ones,' and it has never changed. It's been the same ever since and they appear just as plain today as they did then. God hasn't changed. We're the ones who have changed. Now they come to the mountain because it's a magnetic field, and it's easier for people to be in contact with them. They don't work in just one place; they work all over the world."

She paused. Then she said, "You have to understand what a 'Master' is. A Master was created at the same time that Adam and Eve were created — not at the beginning of the world — at the beginning of the white race. Masters are the children of Elohim. They're not angels. Angels never had physical bodies. Masters were humans once and they ascended; they were the 144,000 that Jesus took up with him when he ascended and he brought them back down to earth to work on the earth until the time of resurrection. It tells you so in the Bible. The trouble is, people don't read the Bible and what it says. They just accept what somebody else says it says."

I knew I must conclude the interview soon, but there were still several questions which needed answers. "Then Jesus brought the 144,000 Ascended Masters back to earth? And that's what 'ascended' means, that they ascended with Jesus?"

"That's right."

"And Jesus also works on earth now?"

"Certainly. He has never left us. He's been here ever since he came to the planet earth."

There was just one more thing I had to know. "If Mt. Shasta is such a point of power, then how will it be affected in the new world you talk about?"

"Mt. Shasta is a seat of understanding. There is less sin and corruption here than in any other part of the earth. That's why you were attracted to the area and that's why I was attracted. All of my interests were in San Jose at one time."

"Do you think that pertains to all the people who live on the slopes of Mt. Shasta?"

"Yes. They're here for a purpose, regardless of who or what they are. There will be more people coming to the slopes of Mt. Shasta, many more," she said, nodding her head.

Reflectively I arose, thanked the gracious lady, and departed. Faded autumn leaves on the path crinkled in the drizzling rain. Closing the gate behind me, I turned and stared at the front door of her home. Nola Van Valer, I thought to myself, is a truly extraordinary woman.

In the late 1960s Garth Sanders of the Redding *Record-Searchlight* (Redding is located about 60 miles south of Mt. Shasta) interviewed Van Valer and she told him about climbing with friends up the east side of the mountain to the 12,451-foot level. She said the area was on the right bank side of Mud Creek. While they were resting, they noticed a very large, black rock formation about 40 feet away from where they sat. And while they were looking at this large rock — because it was unusual — it began to open as if on a pivot. She said they noticed a door leading into a large chamber inside the rock and that it was much like a cavern. They were invited in by a being. The cavern was about 60-feet long and 40-feet wide and down through its center there was a large table which could seat many people. The table appeared to be marble, mostly white with pink and gold threaded through it.

She said the six members of her party were seated at the table and were instructed by a being in a white robe. The being, it turned out, was Phylos the Tibetan. He told the group there were 17 other temples in other parts of the world. And then he explained that his people taught the truth as it was written in the Bible.

So intent were they, Van Valer told Sanders, they did not immediately notice that all around the wall in that large room were standing many other white-robed beings. The walls of the chamber appeared to be made of gold, and there was soft music.

Van Valer went on to explain that she didn't tell of her experiences for a long time because she was afraid curious people would be hurt trying to visit that hazardous slope of Mt. Shasta, and also because she didn't want her experiences to be compared with other reports about Mt. Shasta, some of which she did not approve. She added that she knew nothing about other reported mysterious happenings, and neither did she know anything about the rumored city miles below the peak.

All of her experiences, she said, had been on the McCloud side of the mountain and the experiences were sacred to her.

As for the reported lights on the mountain, even before there were roads, the only explanation she could offer is that the lights came from the auras of the various Masters.

Nola Van Valer passed on some years ago. The Radiant School of the Seekers and Servers continued for a few years, but it no longer exists except in the minds of the former students.

Morning in Mt. Shasta Wonderland — Spring Hill in foreground. Photo by Jim Kottinger.

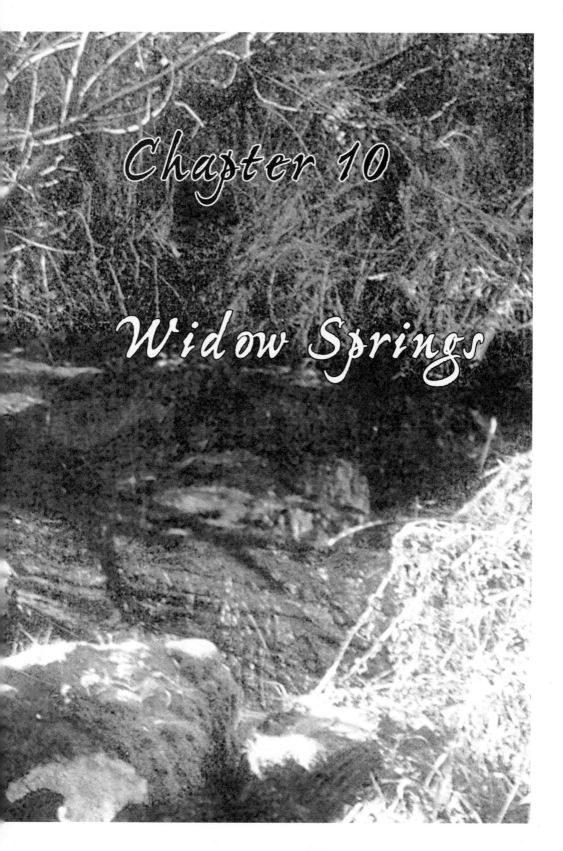

Chapter 10

Widow Springs

Widow Spring's

headwaters,

not

easy to find,

incidentally.

Widow Springs, where Nola Van Valer and her group camped during that period in the 1930s, is on the southeastern slopes of Mt. Shasta and has long been considered by local psychics to be a sacred spot.

Late in November of 1976, just before the snow fell, I went with friends to Widow Springs. It was a memorable day. We had just enjoyed the longest autumn on record and the weather was actually balmy on the mountain. The bracken fern had already turned brown from late autumn frosts but the evergreen forest rose on all sides to a cloudless blue sky.

The area around Widow Springs is well traversed during the summer. Some camp there hoping for a "happening." It has been said this is the place where Godfre Ray King (Guy Ballard, founder of the I Am Activity) first met St. Germain.

Some say the water in Widow Springs is the purest water in the world. Others say the water in the springs contains nine more minerals than any other springwater around. Some say Widow Springs got its name from the Indians; old legends say squaws waited beside the springs for their warriors to return.

Always fascinated by these stories, I welcomed the opportunity to view Widow Springs. I had been in the immediate vicinity before but had never been able to find the springs, even though I had searched for them. I had heard stories of space ships landing in the meadow nearby.

We built a fire (we had a permit) on a flat below the main springs and made some campfire coffee. It was Sunday morning and there a November nip in the air. Waters from the upper spring meandered alongside, and for a long time we savored the fresh coffee and the piney fragrance of the surrounding forest.

The anticipation of seeing the Springs was pleasant, along with the scenery and company.

When, later, we walked the short distance up to the Springs, I was surprised to find how hidden away it was. And how small. But though small, Widow Springs is very unique. It is distinctive in that it has seven tiny whirlpools. They had a rotary motion; a continuous supply of energy is needed to maintain this vortex motion.

The churning waters of Widow Springs are considered to be mystical and the Springs and surrounding area have long been considered a sacred site. A man told me that he heard celestial music while here one morning. And of course, there is Nola Van Valer's reported experiences with Phylos the Tibetan and other notable beings at this same site. She told me that she took 33 people with her who could testify to what she saw and heard.

Reflectively I left Widow Springs and followed my friends through the forest. Shadows were lengthening when, later in the afternoon, we walked up one of the sloping roads toward the peak of Mt. Shasta. A cloud of mist hung along the top of the mountain. The afternoon had a Sunday-stillness to it, and we walked silently, each lost in a sort of reverie. A jet making a perfect white line across the sky brought me back to the present.

We sat on logs beside the road and studied the contours of the great glacier-streaked mountain which rose before us. I wondered just where it was that Nola Van Valer and her friends had found the huge rock-door with "strange writing on it." Did it really exist?

After awhile we turned back. Making sure that our campfire was out, we regretfully left Widow Springs to the snows of winter, deep snows which would hide its seven tiny fountains until the coming spring.

photo by Dick Bliss

Chapter 11

Unveiled Mysteries

What a Cloud!

This is one of the

more

spectacular

lenticular clouds

seen in the area.

The book *Unveiled Mysteries* was published by the Saint Germain Press in 1934 and it contains the author's revelations which began on the slopes of Mt. Shasta. Experienced in the golden autumn of 1930, Godfre Ray King (the pen name under which the late Guy W. Ballard wrote this book and other books) describes his spiritually enlightened introduction into the Brotherhood of Mt. Shasta, a branch of the Great White Lodge. His subsequent and now-famous meeting with Saint Germain on Mt. Shasta is described herewith in his owns words. The following, then, is his most unusual experience exactly as he wrote it:

"Mt. Shasta stood out boldly against the western sky, surrounded at its base by a growth of pine and fir trees that made it look like a jewel of diamond-shining whiteness held in a filigree setting of green. Its snow-covered peak glistened and changed color from moment to moment, as the shadows lengthened in the sun's descent toward the horizon.

"Rumor said there was a group of men – Divine Men in fact – called the Brotherhood of Mt. Shasta, who formed a branch of the Great White Lodge, and that this focus from very ancient times had continued unbroken down to the present day.

"I had been sent on government business to a little town situated at the foot of the mountain, and while thus engaged, occupied my leisure time trying to unravel this rumor concerning The Brotherhood. I knew, through travels in the Far East, that most rumors, myths and legends have, somewhere in their origin, a deep underlying Truth that usually remains unrecognized by all but those who are real students of life.

"I fell in love with Shasta and each morning, almost involuntarily, saluted the Spirit of the Mountain and the Members of the Order. I sensed something very unusual about the entire locality and, in the light of the experiences that followed, I do not wonder that some of them cast their shadows before. Long hikes on the trail had become my habit whenever I wanted to think things out alone or make decisions of serious import. Here, on the great Giant of Nature, I found recreation, inspiration, and peace that soothed my soul and invigorated mind and body.

"I had planned such a hike, for pleasure as I thought, to spend some time deep in the heart of the mountain, when the following experience changed my life so completely that I could almost believe I was on another planet but for my return to the usual routine in which I had been engaged for months.

"The morning in question, I started out at daybreak, deciding to follow where fancy led, and in a vague sort of way, asked God to direct my path. By noon I had climbed high up on the side of the mountain, where the view to the south was beautiful as a dream. As the day advanced, it grew very warm and I stopped frequently to rest and to enjoy to the full the remarkable stretch of country around the McCloud River, valley and town.

"It came time for lunch and I sought a mountain spring for clear, cold water. Cup in hand, I bent down to fill it, when an electrical current passed through my body from head to foot.

"I looked around and directly behind me stood a young man who, at first glance, seemed to be someone on a hike like myself. I looked more closely, and realized immediately that he was no ordinary person. As this thought passed through my mind, he smiled and addressed me saying: 'My Brother, if you will hand me your cup, I will give you a much more refreshing drink than spring water.' I obeyed, and instantly the cup was filled with a creamy liquid. Handing it back to me he said, 'Drink it.'

"I did so, and must have looked astonished. The taste was delicious, but the electrical vivifying effect in my mind and body made me gasp with surprise. I did not see him put anything into the cup and I wondered how it happened.

'That which you drank,' he explained, 'comes directly from the Universal Supply, pure and vivifying as Life Itself, in fact it is Life — Omnipresent Life — for it exists everywhere about us. It is the subject to our conscious control and direction, willingly obedient when we Love enough, because all the Universe obeys the behest of Love. Whatsoever I desire manifests itself, when I command in Love. I held out the cup, and that which I desired for you appeared. See! I have but to hold out my hand and, if I wish to use gold — gold is here.' Instantly, there lay in his palm a disc about the size of a ten dollar gold-piece.

"Again he continued: 'I see within you a certain inner understanding of the Great Law, but you are not outwardly aware of It enough to produce that which you desire direct from the Omnipresent Universal Supply. You have desired to see something of this kind so intensely, so honestly, and so determinedly, it could not longer be withheld from you.

"'However, precipitation is one of the least important activities of the Great Truth of Being. If your desire had not been free from selfishness and the fascination of phenomena, such an experience could not have come to you. When leaving home this morning you thought you were coming on a hike, that is, so far as the outer activity of your mind was concerned. In the deeper, larger sense you were really following the urge of your Inner God Self that led to the person, place, and condition wherein your intense desire could be fulfilled.

"'The Truth of Life is, you cannot desire that which is not possible of manifestation somewhere in the Universe. The more intense the feeling within the desire, the more quickly it will be attained. However, if one be foolish enough to desire something that will injure another of God's children, or any other part of His Creation, then that person will pay the penalty in discord and failure somewhere in his own Life's experience.

"'It is very important to realize fully that God's intent for every one of His children is abundance of every good and perfect thing. He created Perfection and endowed His children with exactly the same power. They can create and maintain Perfection also, and express God-Dominion over the earth and all that is therein. Mankind was originally created in the Image and Likeness of God. The only reason all do not manifest Dominion is because they do not use their Divine Authority — that with which each individual is endowed and by which he is intended to govern his world. Thus, they are not obeying the Law of Love by pouring out peace and blessing to all creation.

"'This comes about through their failure to accept and acknowledge themselves as Temples of the Most High Living God, and to hold this acknowledgement with eternal recognition. Humanity, in its present seeming limitation of time, space and activity, is in the same condition a person in need would be to whom someone held out a handful of money. If the needy one did not step forward and accept the money held out to him, how in the world could he ever have the benefit which it could bring?

"'The mass of mankind is exactly in this state of consciousness today and will continue in it until they accept the God within their hearts as the Owner, Giver, and Doer of all the Good that has ever come into their lives and world. The personal self of every individual must acknowledge completely and unconditionally that the human or outer activity of consciousness has absolutely nothing of its own. Even the energy by which one recognizes the Great God within is radiated into the personal self by the Great God Self.

"'Love and praise of the Great Self Within and the attention maintained focused upon Truth, health, freedom, peace, supply, or any other thing that you may desire for right use, persistently held in your conscious thought and feeling, will bring them into your use and world, as surely as there is a Great Law of Magnetic Attraction in the Universe.

"'The Eternal Law of Life is: What you think and feel you bring into form; where your thought is there you are, for you are your consciousness; and what you meditate upon, you become.'"

After gently but eloquently presenting the truths of the great eternal law of life to Ballard, Saint Germain reveals his identity, first asking him to remain still for a few moments. "I did as he requested," wrote Ballard, "and in perhaps a full minute I saw his face, body and clothing become the living, breathing, tangible 'Presence' of the Master, Saint Germain, smiling at my astonishment and enjoying my surprise.

"He stood there before me — a magnificent God-like figure — in a white jeweled robe, a Light and Love sparkling in his eyes that revealed and proved the Dominion and Majesty that are his.

Saint Germain explained, "This is the body in which I work a great deal of the time when occupied with the welfare of mankind, unless the work I am doing at the moment requires closer contact with the outer world of affairs, and in that case, I make my body take on the characteristics and dress of the nation with which I am working at the moment."

Then Saint Germain devoted much time explaining further beneficial work done by those who had attained the Ascended State, not only in America but all over the world, saying that they were capable of controlling the atomic structure of the entire world and that unfortunately, through misuse, lack of understanding, or mental inertia, mankind had placed restrictions upon themselves which prohibits the same powers.

He then instructed Ballard to return to their trysting place on Mt. Shasta at seven o'clock the following morning.

The author relates in the book, "Light of heart, I was soon on my way, determined not to miss any opportunity to ask questions, if permitted. As I approached the appointed place, my body became lighter and lighter until by the time I was within a quarter of a mile, my feet scarcely touched the ground. There was no one in sight so I sat down on a log to wait for Saint Germain, feeling no fatigue whatsoever, although my hike had been about ten miles.

"As I contemplated the wonderful privilege and blessing that had come to me, I heard a twig crack and looked around, expecting to see him. Imagine my surprise, when not 50 feet away, I saw a panther − slowing approaching. My hair must have stood on end. I wanted to run, to scream − anything − so frantic was the feeling of fear within me. It would have been useless to move, for one spring from the panther would have been fatal to me.

"My brain whirled so great was my fear, but one idea came through clearly and held my attention steady. I realized that I had the Mighty 'Presence of God' right within me and that this 'Presence' was all love. This beautiful animal was a part of God's Life also and I made myself look at it, directly in the eyes. Then came the thought, that one part of God could not harm another part. I was conscious of this fact only.

"A feeling of Love swept over me and went out like a Ray of Light directly to the panther and with it went my fear. The stealthy tread ceased and I moved slowly toward it, feeling that God's love filled us both. The vicious glare in the eyes softened, the animal straightened up and came slowly to me, rubbing its shoulder against my leg. I reached down and stroked the soft head. It looked up into my eyes for a moment and then, lay down and rolled over like a playful kitten. The fur was a beautiful dark reddish-brown − the body long, supple and of great strength. I continued to play with it and when I suddenly looked up, Saint Germain stood beside me."

According to the author, Saint Germain said, "My son, I saw the great strength within you or I would not have permitted so great a test. You have conquered fear. My congratulations! Had you not conquered the outer-self, I would not have allowed the panther to harm you but our association would have ceased for a time.

"I did not have anything to do with the panther being there. It was part of the Inner operation of the Great Law, as you will see before the association with your new-found friend ceases. Now that you have passed the test of courage, it is possible for me to give much greater assistance. Each day you will become stronger, happier, and express much greater freedom."

Whereupon, Saint Germain seated himself beside Ballard and the instruction began.

During the next weeks, Ballard continued to meet St. Germain, receiving encouragement, strength, and instruction which would prepare him for his future role assisting humanity upon this earth.

I, as a writer, cannot begin to convey the complete message brought forth in the book *Unveiled Mysteries* — the above was only the beginning. But the author reveals a prophecy which was unfolded to him — that the earth has entered a new era, the Golden Crystal Age, and the sinister force attempting to create chaos and destruction throughout the world will be destroyed. When that is accomplished, the mass of humanity will turn to the "Great God Presence" within each heart, the Presence which also governs the universe. Peace shall reign on earth, and man will send out good will to man. Furthermore, he states in the foreword of the book: "To those who read this work, I wish to say that these experiences are as real and true as mankind's existence on this earth today, and that they all occurred during August, September and October of 1930, upon Mt. Shasta, California, U.S.A."

Chapter 12

Sphinx Rock

The huge stone face looks out over

the slopes of Mt. Shasta

and is located at a level of about

11,000 feet.

At the base of Sphinx Rock

is the head of Clear Creek.

Nearby are numerous

snow fields and Wintun Glacier.

On the lighter side, there is that phenomenon called Sphinx Rock which can be seen on the slopes of Mt. Shasta.

When you see this strange formation, you will wonder about it. Is it the handiwork of nature? Is it a carving of some ancient tribesmen? Or is it, indeed, the work of the Lemurians, those fabled inhabitants of the mystic mountain?

Sphinx Rock was discovered and named by the late Frank Bascom, who was also instrumental in discovering the mysterious petroglyphs of Castle Crags, ancient granite spires a few miles south of Mt. Shasta (discussed in the following chapter).

The story of Sphinx Rock is rather strange, indeed. Bascom liked to hike on the upper slopes of Mt. Shasta, and he always took his camera. One day he was photographing the sulphur springs near the top of the mountain and also other odd formations when he unknowingly snapped a picture of Sphinx Rock.

The next day he was developing his prints and in one of them he saw an awesome face on a huge boulder. He became very excited about it and went back up the mountain the next day to hunt for the strange face. He made a step-by-step survey of the entire region in which he thought he had snapped that particular photograph, to no avail. Alas, there were many rocks and boulders and not one was like the boulder that had materialized in his prints.

After much searching on other days, once accompanied by Dr. O. A. Herzog, Professor of Languages at the University of Minnesota, Bascom finally located the boulder on the point of a ridge which faces due south in Clear Creek Canyon.

When he studied what he now called "Sphinx Rock," he noted that the huge face looking out over the slopes of Mt. Shasta was located at about the 11,000-foot level.

If anyone would like a close look at this unique formation, it is located about one-half mile northwesterly from Mud Creek. (Clear Creek, which supplies Mud Creek with much of its water, heads at the base of Sphinx Rock, and there are snowfields nearby, with Wintun the nearest glacier.)

Those who have seen it say the features on the face are easily distinguishable and the boulder can be sighted from a distance.

Was Sphinx Rock carved eons ago by a member of a prehistoric race? Was it carved by local Indians? Was it carved by nature?

Who knows? Sphinx Rock is just another mystery on Mt. Shasta, a bewitching mountain which seems to beckon to those searching for adventure, mystery, and intrigue.

photo courtesy Roy Haile

Chapter 13

The Baffling Castle Crags Petroglyphs

There's supposed to be

gold

up there in those

jagged spires

of Castle Crags,

but you will probably

never find it.

*I*n an area where mystery is omnipresent, here is yet another perplexing and unsolved puzzle of the ages: the Castle Crags petroglyphs, discovered several decades ago by two Dunsmuir high school students and the late Frank Bascom.

Castle Crags, just south of Mt. Shasta, is ages older than the ancient mountain itself. These glacier-polished crags are unrelated to the more recent volcanic activity of the mountain and are made up of granitic material which was formed some 225 million years ago far beneath the surface of the earth and later forced slowly upward through a blanket of serpentine and glacial debris by a process of fold-faulting.

Castle Crags, with its towering spires and domes, is surrounded by primitive back-country and is now one of California's most enchanting state parks. A scenic overlook high within the park boasts an overall view that is literally staggering in its beauty — magnificent canyons far below, still-unspoiled whitewater rivers, alpine lakes, and to the north glacier-streaked Mt. Shasta looms, 14,162 feet of incredible brilliance.

Flowing through the lower slopes of Castle Crags is Little Castle Creek and it was in this area that the high school boys were hiking one sunny day. Tarrying awhile beside a huge cleft boulder, one of them casually brushed aside some loose material and was startled to find the impression of a human hand on the boulder, a man's hand. The imprint had been chiseled into the granite and filled with a red cement-like solution, used apparently for the purpose of keeping any growth of vegetation from covering the symbol.

Excitedly they hunted for more carvings and nearby found two more symbols, serpentine in form. Then on the opposite side of the boulder, they found another hand, smaller and more delicately moulded, which obviously represented a female hand.

Hurrying home to relate their mysterious find, they returned shortly with Frank Bascom, who was associated with the U. S. Forest Service and also dabbled in archaeology and geology. The boys led the way up Castle Creek canyon, on up the Mount Bradley road, then hiked along the banks of Castle Creek. Finally the threesome reached the graven rock. More searching revealed, in a willow clump, a second set of carvings which included two Maltese cross designs — one created in a zigzag line decorated with dots and the other composed of two E-like characters.

Intrigued, Bascom immediately reported the discovery to the Shasta National Forest officials and a third trip was made to the site. More carvings were found nearby. On a rock upstream, which measured about eight feet in height, were found a male and female hand and more petroglyphs. The palm of the male hand bore an engraving similar to a capital E, and the female hand bore a curious double triangle symbol. On the opposite side of the boulder they found the likeness of a bovine head.

Female hand with double triangular symbols.

Male hand with 'E'-like symbol

The Castle Crags petroglyphs include a male hand, a female hand, two symbols (serpentine in form), two Maltese Cross designs (one created in a zigzag line decorated with dots), two E-like characters. The palm of the male hand bears an engraving similar to a capital E, the female hand bears a curious double triangle symbol (see opposite page, bottom picture, left-most symbols). Also (not pictured) a beautifully shaped woman's hand in whose palm is chiseled a symbol of the four rivers of life.

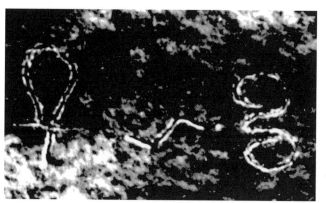

The symbol of life, and characters similar to ancient greek letters 'N' and 'K'.

Bascom, certain that they had made an important discovery, returned to the area accompanied by George Schrader (who represented the local U. S. Forest Supervisor) and other personnel from the U. S. Forest Service. This group investigated the fascinating petroglyphs. Bascom then wrote an article about the Castle Creek experiences in which he stated:

"The fact stands out that the petroglyphs or symbols chiseled in the coarse granite rocks up Castle Creek show greater skill and symmetry and a higher degree of culture than any found elsewhere in different places of southwestern United States. The petroglyphs have been colored a reddish hue with some unknown liquid solution, and it was evidently used to keep any growth of vegetation from covering the symbols.

"The people who did this work were no doubt artists possessing great skill. On what is now two large boulders there was at some remote time, one huge rock which at some time was cleft asunder. The symbols are on the east side of these two rocks. Those on the rock to the south reveal a large man's hand, painted with some unknown stain. In the palm of the hand is chiseled the "all-seeing eye" and on the rock to the north is a beautifully-shaped woman's hand in whose palm is chiseled a form of the swastika (which is thought to be a very ancient symbol of the four rivers of life, or eternity; the swastika symbol is pre-Christian in origin and was found in the ruins of the lost continent of Lemuria (Mu) as well as in India, China and Tibet).

"Were the symbols placed on the two rocks before or after the rock broke and separated? On the rock to the north, the woman's hand is at the side and not in the center of the rock. In chiseling the rock, the natural thing would be to place such work in the center and not at the side of the rock. This might indicate that the symbols were cut into the rock prior to its separation."

On the heels of these remarkable petroglyph discoveries came various interpretations. Letters were exchanged with the Department of Anthropology at the University of California; communications came from authorities at Stanford University; and from the Academy Press in New Jersey came a letter to Frank Bascom from Alvin Boyd Kuhn stating that he thought the symbols had been chiseled into the boulders by local Indians.

Bascom replied: "This I doubt. In talking with the highest type of the older local Indians, they state this work was not chiseled by Indians. Therefore, we have to turn to another source. Dr. Julian Stewart shows in his book *Petroglyphs of the United States* (which sets forth all the petroglyphs found in this country by Indians) that the Indian and the Maya civilization started from a Lemurian colony have stated that the Maya used ferric oxide, a red pigment, to deter erosion, and the pigment on the petroglyphs could be the same."

Bascom added, "Churchward, in his 'Lost Continent of Mu' lists six of the symbols found at Castle Crags: the swastika, a form of the Maltese cross, the triangle, the all-seeing eye, the serpent and the three steps to the throne. He found these symbols engraved on clay tablets in the temples of India as they had existed in the sunken continent of Mu and I'd consider them authentic."

And so the controversy continued. Considering the age of Castle Crags, local persons including Bascom insisted that these mystic signs were carved into the granite rock in a prehistoric era, and these theories are supported by those who believe that Mt. Shasta area is, indeed, part of the last remaining portion of the vast continent of Lemuria which sank into the Pacific Ocean together with most of its ancient, advanced and highly skilled civilization.

The Castle Crags petroglyphs still remain a mystery. Who carved the delicate, intricate symbols into the hard, granite boulders and when and why will probably always be just another mystery in an area where mysteries abound.

The dome on the extreme right is called "po-tal-lie-shun" by the Indians. Giant's dome, or Castle dome is isolated from the main group of the crags and rises 4,966 feet high.

photo courtesy of Neil and Carl Clement

Chapter 14

A Race Of "Little Men" On Mt. Shasta

The tiny men began to sing,

seeming to

blend their voices

in a chorus of beautiful

cosmic sounds —

all the while working with

tiny anvils and hammers.

Mt. Shasta will always bask in the aura of occult legends. And those who have viewed the mountain have said that there are no rivals to match her beauty, grace, and symmetry. It is certain, too, that Mt. Shasta has no other rival to match her mysteries.

The following is a story which has been around a long time. From the 1953 issue of the *Siskiyou Pioneer* published by the Siskiyou County Historical Society, comes a poignant tale written by the late Alex J. Rosborough, one of Siskiyou County's most distinguished citizens.

As usual, his story is strange and flavored with mystery:

"Out of the tangle of stories told about 'Ieka' (the great white mountain) and the still-clinging beliefs by many that a race of little men dwelt around its slopes prior to the coming of the Indians, and that along its miles and miles of lava-born sides — filled with cracks and caverns — some still survive, let's pick out this one in keeping with Christmas gladness and joy.

"Not far from the base of old Ieka was a home where a little child, wracked with the pain of infantile paralysis, lay restless and sobbing — the bones of her left shoulder being gradually twisted into deformity by the dreaded and seemingly uncheckable disease. Everything the good old doctor could suggest and all the kind and loving treatment by her parents availed nought.

"Tomorrow would be Christmas. The doctor had promised to come again to see her on that day, and Uncle Ray had already arrived to be with his folks and to see his little niece, bringing with him a 'something' wrapped in a mink skin, which he seemed to care about very much.

"Uncle Ray was a big and powerfully built man. He was a trapper and spent much of his time among the Indians, bartering for pelts and running his trap lines in winter on snowshoes. These lines took him across the great slopes of Mt. Shasta, to the heads of the Sacramento and McCloud rivers, to Butte and Antelope creeks and into Shasta Valley. He lived much with the Indians, learned their talk, listened to their stories.

"One day, to a large gathering of the tribe who came from far and near to celebrate the opening of their fishing season, came a very old Indian in whom Uncle Ray became very interested because he seemed to be familiar with early times, long before the white man came. In listening to the old chief telling of his experiences in boyhood days, one story in particular impressed Uncle Ray — it related to the old Indian having run across a very small footprint high up on Mt. Shasta (the chief called the mountain Ieka) while tracking a panther. This small and apparently human track led him across a wide pumice slope – and then the footprint was lost in the rocks below a high cliff of lava flow.

"Many times on his trap trail, the trapper pondered over the incident related by the white-haired Indian. While never once doubting the veracity of the chief's statement, he nevertheless was semi-convinced that there might have been some mistake about the track. Always alert as to the description and location of the lava rock cliff as indicated and marked on the sand by his Indian friend, he found, at last, a mass of rocks which had in times long past run out as molten lava.

"The trapper managed, by a circular climb, to reach the top of the cliff, where he almost stepped into a deep hole in the rock – the hole was barely large enough to admit a man's body. Lighting a couple of small pitch sticks which he always carried in his pocket to start a fire, Uncle Ray began to explore a big, dry cavern room.

"Christmas Eve had come and as it neared the midnight hour, Uncle Ray went to his pack of rare furs and picked out something wrapped in a mink skin and then laid a small, beautifully-made stone doll on the arm of the pain-wracked, suffering child. Then he withdrew from the room.

"As the big old grandfather clock gonged its twelve o'clock, Mama, Papa, Uncle Ray and the doctor peeped in through the half-open door to wish the little crippled girl a 'Merry Christmas' – but Mama hushed them with a warning finger for the child was sitting up in bed with her little stone doll clasped in her good arm, and with what had been her helpless arm raised high she smiled at them through grateful tears and softly sang, 'Glory to God on high and peace on earth to men of good will.'"

It would seem, considering the above touching story, that the old legends of Mt. Shasta's "little men" are still being told. Another interesting experience relating to little men inhabiting Mt. Shasta is recorded in a book *Lord Maitreya, or the New Golden Age* written by Mah-Atmah Amsumata, otherwise known as Norman R. Westfall.

Westfall describes the incident in a segment of his book entitled "The King of Lemuria" and the curious happening unfolded one day in late spring, over forty years ago.

According to the author, he and two companions, Jesse and Elizabeth, walked up the alpine road north of the city of Mount Shasta, a road which led to the peak of Mt. Shasta. It was a beautiful day in May and the group had planned a picnic at a lovely site he had discovered earlier in the week. Turning right about a half-mile up the road, they followed a new road that angled to the right, past what he calls Krishna's Well. Finding a secluded area beneath the giant pines, they tarried a while to enjoy a basket of fruit.

They had barely settled themselves on the soft blanket of pine needles, he wrote, when a tiny dwarf appeared and asked Jesse if she would like for him to bring her some gold, adding that there was much gold in the mountain. He then disappeared and soon returned with a sack of what appeared to be coal. The dwarf explained, however, that the sack contained black diamonds and that within them lay a secret.

Westfall relates that they suddenly realized that this was a dwarf of vast wisdom, and strangely enough, other dwarfs appeared and explained that they were from the lost continent of Lemuria. The tiny men began to sing, seeming to blend their voices in a chorus of beautiful cosmic sounds — all the while working with tiny anvils and hammers. One dwarf, working near Elizabeth, reportedly created a golden ring which he presented to her.

Then, amazingly, there appeared another being, somewhat larger than the others. Lordlike in appearance, he introduced himself as Pelleur, the Lord of Wisdom of Lemuria, the Great Dwarf who sits in the center of the four corners of the earth. He said further, according to Westfall, that the four angels of the four corners of the earth were his servants and that the four angels represented earth, water, air, and fire. He added that it was he who brought to them the rough diamonds and that the four angels of the four corners of the earth would help them produce the finished diamond, the sun.

He then reportedly raised his hand and presented to Jesse a golden chain, the last link upon which was inscribed the symbol of the sanskrit (Aum).

After making the group his disciples, he vanished, and the threesome walked slowly back to the village of Mount Shasta, pondering the things they had seen and heard that day.

Later in the same month, Westfall states that he and Jesse made the same two-mile walk up the mountain road and returned to the sequestered place beneath the pines, pausing first near Krishna's Well to scatter some holy rice as they had been advised to do. The act was symbolic of the blessing of the Great Lord and also part of a certain ceremonial initiation. Again there appeared a dwarf, and also one described in the book as the Great Mahatma Koot Hoomi. Then Mahatma Koot Hoomi, Jesse, and Westfall formed a blessed union, according to the author, after which they were advised by the Lord of Wisdom of Lemuria that through love they would command, and that all things in all worlds are created through love. They were directed to go quickly to perform the work of perfection in the bodies, minds, brains, and spirits of all human beings in all realms of life.

Chapter 15

Mysterious
Circles & Mounds,
Pyramids & Domes

Black Butte

was originally named

"Muirs Peak"

by famed naturalist

John Muir.

The afternoon I interviewed Nola Van Valer, I noticed a curious publication on her table and I asked if I could borrow it. She didn't mind. The name of it was *Gnostica News* and included in it was an article entitled "Mount Shasta, America's Holy Mountain" authored by Richard L. Tierney.

Tierney wrote about odd mounds in the immediate area around Mt. Shasta. He stated that he had turned off a road near Black Butte and saw some strange mounds beside the road. Stopping to look at them closely, he found them to be strangely regular, perhaps 30 feet high and covered with scrub brush, with here and there a large tree growing out the side. He climbed two of the mounds, which seemed to be made of piled-up rocks. If this were Mexico, he noted, instead of northern California, they could be unexcavated pyramids or temple platforms. The only other explanation he gave for these curious mounds was that they could have been tailing piles from mines, but he had never heard of any mineshafts in that particular area.

In 1970, on another January trip to the area, he drove to Weed and explored the countryside between that city and Dwinnell Reservoir (which is now Lake Shastina). He had read about some unusual stone rings in the *Division of Mines Bulletin 151:* "Geology of the Macdoel Quadrangle," and he said he had found a large number of the rings where the road crossed a long, low ridge just north of Edgewood. They were about 50 feet in diameter and very slightly raised above the level of the ground; that is, the bare ground within each circle of stones was humped up like a very shallow dome.

According to Tierney, he counted about 24 such circles, and he said that there were many more. They seemed to continue on down the boulder-strewn ridge indefinitely. He noted there was not much variation in the size of the rings: the stones marking their boundaries ranged from head-size to golf-ball size and the width of the boundary was a yard or two. He didn't see much vegetation in the area, only stunted grass and tiny range plants and even those were sparse. He thought the rock type was basalt.

Driving back to the city of Mount Shasta, he stopped again to investigate the strange stone mounds he had found west of Black Butte. Most of them were overgrown with scrub brush, but others had large trees growing atop them.

These, he thought, were fairly old. They seemed to be composed of boulders, about head-size or larger. He saw no evidence of worked stone, yet the overall impression he received was one of artificiality. They resembled unexcavated temple mounds he had seen in Mexico. Were they tailing piles from the previous century, he wondered. He had seen no pits, however. Were they small, highly-weathered volcanic plugs? Neither of these explanations seemed satisfactory to him. He stated that he preferred to think that they are the remains of the structures of a prehistoric race.

In March of the same year he returned to the Lake Shastina area and snapped some photographs of the peculiar rings. While doing so, he paced off the diameters of five of the circles and found them all to be very close to sixty feet across. There were, he said, dozens of the rings atop the ridge for as far as he could see, all about the same diameter.

On the way back to the city of Mount Shasta, he stopped to photograph a couple of the mounds near Black Butte. Unfortunately, not one of the pictures came out. He said his camera shutter had jammed immediately.

And, of course, he blamed it on the Lemurians.

Interestingly enough, I had read of other mounds such as these in the realm of Mt. Shasta, and the origin of these mounds is unknown. There are also a number of stone circles near Leaf which had geologists in a quandary some years ago. Leaf is about half-way between Grass Lake and Tennant.

The circles at Leaf surround slight mounds about 60 feet across and 2- to 3-feet high. They're located on a knoll and they're well-covered by sagebrush. These circles consist of stones of all shapes and sizes and lie in a shallow ditch about 1-foot deep by 2-feet wide. The ditches are filled with rock just to the surface of the surrounding areas and give the appearance of a stone pavement or mosaic.

The stones in the bottom are round-edged, about the size of a potato. The stones above are larger and irregular. On the surface of the ground outside the circles are more irregularly-sized rocks.

The very first issue of the *Siskiyou Pioneer*, published in 1946 by the Siskiyou County Historical Society, mentioned these odd circle formations and stated: "Examination of aerial photographs revealed that the circles not only were clearly visible but they roughly covered nearly 600 acres in four tracts in the area immediately surrounding Leaf."

On a field trip to investigate the circles, accompanied by Etna geologist Burton J. Westman, excavations in one or two of the mounds were negative insofar as finding anything relating to human origin. The investigation revealed, however, that within the mounds themselves there were no rocks above the surface level of the surrounding ground — this was considered to be peculiar, considering the rocky terrain.

Westman made a detailed report in which he expressed belief that the rock circles were "cultural" and had to be because he had never heard of, nor had he ever seen, a similar natural phenomenon. Not long after that, the University of California Museum of Anthropology decided to investigate. After a careful exploration, reports by their group were negative insofar as human origin of the circles was concerned. They said, "Show us one artifact and we will believe they are human, but we have never seen or heard of any man-made structures of this kind."

At that time other scientists who had merely read the reports thought the stone circles at Leaf might be "Brodel circles." These are caused by frost action under certain circumstances over a long period of time. Though Brodel circles turn up frequently in the Yukon area, this peculiar formation has never been recognized as far south as Leaf.

Furthermore, other scientists were not so sure that the Leaf circles were Brodel circles or rings because those circles, on such a tremendous scale, were an unknown phenomena.

And so the mounds and circles of Edgewood, Leaf, and the Black Butte area still remain a mystery. Do these strange formations have anything at all to do with the controversial and mystic mountain which rises so majestically above them? No one seems to know.

In the fall of 1988 another very mysterious rock design on the north slope of Mt. Shasta was discovered by the United States Forest Service and has been monitored ever since.

The huge design, which covers an area the size of a football field, consists of individual rocks lined into shapes: a triangle with a circle at each point. Within each circle is a six-pointed star. In one circle is a circle of rocks and a circle of stones with incense nearby.

The area surrounding it is immaculately clean and the design is so perfect that Forest Service officials think it must have been laid out with surveying tools or string. The Forest Service district ranger thought the area could be a gathering place for New Agers, and also said that it was possible that the rock design was laid out during the Harmonic Convergence of 1987. Pre-Harmonic Convergence aerial photos do not show the rock design.

While it appears that people worship there, daily fly-overs conducted prior to the full moon in July, 1989, showed no arrivals at the site. Further investigation of the rock design revealed a suggestion for the significance of the six-pointed stars which are part of the design. A six-pointed star is actually two triangles laid pointing opposite directions. Furthermore, meditation on a triangle with the point facing up provides the spiritual, heavenly aspect, while meditation on a triangle pointed down provides the practical, earthly aspect of life. And finally, meditation on the six-pointed star creates a balance.

J. E. Cirlot's *Dictionary of Symbols* states that the six-pointed star is said to be a symbol of the human soul.

Others say the combination of triangles to form a six-pointed star represents fire and water, spirit and matter, man and woman — the conjunction of opposites. Contained within a circle — totality.

As of this writing, the United States Forest Service has not decided what to do about the strange rock design, if anything, except continue to monitor the site because it is located in the Mt. Shasta Wilderness Area and there are wilderness regulations. For instance, rules prevent organized gatherings of more than 25 people in a wilderness area, and it's against the rules to set up a man-made facility or to conduct a money-making activity without a permit. So far, there have been no large crowds there, and so far there has been no explanation as to its origin.

Mysteries, mysteries. They're all part of the great white mountain which is attracting more and more curiosity seekers and mystic pilgrims to its slopes.

Consider the Kriya Yoga pilgrims, reportedly devoted followers of the Great Tamil Yoga Siddha-Adept, Kriya Babaji Nagharaj. Each year, it is said, these pilgrims (who represent International Kriya Babaji Yoga Sangam) make a pilgrimage to Mt. Shasta, which to them is sacred and symbolic of the Great Yoga Siddhanta ideal of immortality.

Following ancient traditions of mysticism pioneered in south India, these pilgrims reputedly travel on foot through 60 miles of dense forests to worship Shasta Ayyappa Swami, son of Yogi Shiva and Lord Conquer of the negative forces. (Yoga students worship him intensively for 48 days according to ancient Tamil Yoga traditions and undertake this pilgrimage in India, and now in America.)

Inspired by Kriya Babaji, Yogi Ramaiah has established a mystic shrine on Shasta Ayyappa Swami at the seventh milestone on the Everitt Memorial Highway near the junction of Old Wagon Camp Road. The shrine consists of four pyramids with plaques which sanctify Kriya Yogic practices. These include the chanting of biji mantras in tune with Divine Nature, which reaches its zenith of beauty there on the sylvan slopes of Mt. Shasta — whose eternal cloak of white snow is symbolic of the white light which Kriya Yoga Sadhaks experience in the spiritual plane. Their shrine of pyramids is designed to provide an atmosphere where the disciples chant and pray in meditation to the Great Divine Holy Intelligence to render a purifying blessing to the world.

Thousands have become familiar with the mystic mountain throughout the years. Many hike the slopes of the mountain because they believe it to be sacred, while others are attracted by the mysteries which seem to grow and multiply with the years. Forest Service personnel have found wooden crosses, mystic symbols carved on trees and rocks, and marble slabs anchored in cement with shrine-like inscriptions.

And was she hallucinating or did Lynn Ferrin really see a colorful scene on the mountain? Ferrin wrote in the 1971 July/August issue of *Motorland* magazine that she had been climbing the talus slopes above Horse Camp. The day was warm and the climb strenuous. She sat down to rest. Then she noticed something very strange. On top of a butte in the distance, someone had pitched a splendid tent.

Ferrin said it looked like an ornate medieval pavilion with white silken flaps riffling in the breeze. Below the tent the cliff dropped away almost vertically.

She sat there lost in admiration. And wonder. How in the world could a person have gotten that thing up there? She decided it could only have been the work of some imaginative hippies and started climbing again.

Glancing back minutes later, she was astonished to find it had vanished.

In 1955, John W. Chamberlin, Yreka newspaperman, led an expedition on Mt. Shasta in an effort to either substantiate reports that a prehistoric race did live on or in the mountain, or to dispel the myths forever. Hoping to discover some old ruins, he found instead enormous footprints measuring 15 inches long. The distance between footprints measured about 50 inches, indicating that the elusive creature must weigh at least 450 pounds.

Curiously, the feet that had left the print in the loose dirt had only three toes, and the prints also had what seemed to be two knobby depressions at the heel, which Chamberlin said could have been heavy callouses.

After apprehensively trailing the footprints from approximately the 11,500-foot level to more than 1,500 feet up the mountain, the party discontinued the search. But their experience naturally resulted in more publicity and the subsequent tongue-in-cheek presumption that the huge footprints belonged to a three-toed Lemurian, or to one of the "old ones."

Then there is the story of Professor Edgar Lucin Larkin, Director of Mount Lowe Observatory in southern California some years ago as told by Wishar S. Cerve (pseudonym for H. Spencer Lewis) in his book *Lemuria — The Lost Continent of the Pacific*.

Professor Larkin, it seems, was experimenting with a new feature of one of the long-distance telescopes, turning it north and south of his location along the top of the mountain range upon which the observatory was located, merely for the purpose of testing a new standard scale for determining distances.

He chose Mt. Shasta as an object upon which to focus his vision at this particular testing time because, he said, through this long-distance telescope the high snow-capped peaks of Mt. Shasta stood out clearly against the deep blue sky.

"After he had consulted the maps of California," the author wrote, "and determined in miles and feet the exact distance between himself and the peak of Shasta, and made his notations for the purpose of comparing these figures with the new scale of relative distances upon which he was working, he moved the telescope so that its field of vision included lower portions of the sides of Shasta, and anticipating that he would see only the tops of trees in the foreground, he was surprised to see a glimmering curved surface that was truly unusual in any picture anticipated by him."

Cerve continues: "As the sun shone upon this glittering object among the trees, he was impressed with the thought that he was looking at a gold-tinted dome of some Oriental building. At various intervals, 20 minutes apart, he made further notations and as the sun moved in its course he was impressed that there were two domes rising above the treetops near Shasta and that a part of the third one could be seen several hundred feet distant. Moving the telescope once again he found visible between the trees a corner of another structure seemingly made of marble. Knowing that there were no such structures in northern California and especially in the land around Shasta, he left his telescope fixed to see what these things would look like in the setting sun and in darkness. He was surprised to find later in the night great lights around this dome, apparently white, which partially illuminated and made them visible even though there was no moon to cast any light at the time."

"In his usual precise way," author Cerve wrote, "he made careful notations regarding each peculiar thing that impressed his mind and waited for sunrise to make further observations. Another adjustment of the telescope permitted him to see smoke rising between the trees and likewise to see part of another structure. After one week's study of the matter he decided to investigate further and it was his investigation, personally conducted, that led many persons to explore the region as was found possible. Such is the story told by Larkin's friends."

Several paragraphs later Cerve described unusual ceremonies performed by mysterious people inhabiting Mt. Shasta:

"Those who have seen some of them at their midnight ceremony around the fire claim that they have seen the silhouettes of some four or five hundred figures, and that this number represents only a fraction of those grouped on one side of the fire. The origin of the fire or its nature is not known. It does not appear to be the burning of wood or brush or of even oil or gasoline, for it is a very white light almost bordering upon a violet blueness in its brilliancy.

"At one part of the midnight ceremony beams of bright lights are cast upward into the trees, often blazing in the sky and occasionally tinging the edge of a cloud that may be hanging low. These beams of light strike against the upper portions of buildings and particularly on the domes that seem to be plated with gold. Where the buildings are illuminated and can be observed at all they appear to be constructed of marble and onyx. At sunrise another similar ceremony is conducted, attracting a great deal of attention because of the lights that appear in the darkest parts of the forest.

"The only key to these ceremonies that has ever been found is that which was carved upon a stone and set up near the outskirts of the forest as stelai were erected in Egypt. On one of these there were a number of hieroglyphics and underneath were cut in a careful manner the English words, 'Ceremony of Adoration to Guatama.' The hieroglyphics indicated that the ceremony referred to was performed at sunrise, sunset, and midnight — and that the word 'Guatama' means the continent of America. An adoration ceremony of this kind would be taken to mean a celebration of appreciation, and this, therefore, must be in honor of the time when the forebears of these mysterious people were saved from the great catastrophe by coming to this mountainous region of Lemuria as it was submerging."

Chapter 16

Acquainted With
A Shasta Night

"You've heard these stories

about the mountain", says Corder.

"I'm not much a believer about the

supernatural, but I'll tell you,

we had a helping hand.

And it's not our imagination."

Strange stories have been told by people who have spent the night, or part of it, on the slopes of Mt. Shasta. The following is such a story. It was written by my friend Lee Juillerat of the *Klamath Falls Herald and News* in the September 27, 1981, edition, and is reprinted here with his permission:

It was 9:30 p.m. and the night sky was lit with stars. But Don Corder and his hiking companion were in no mood for gazing. They were tired, weary, and anxious.

The day had begun ominously enough before sunrise when their wind-up clock stopped ticking only minutes before the alarm was supposed to jangle them awake. Still, they had risen early enough to gulp a quick breakfast, strap on their packs, and begin their trek in the aerial darkness from Horse Camp to the 13,000-plus-foot saddle on Whitney Glacier between Shastina and Mt. Shasta's summit. Looking back, Corder wonders about his companion's flashlight, which, even with fresh batteries, broadcast only a dim beam.

The climb up to the Whitney had been arduous. They'd spent the day searching and probing the wreckage of a twin-engine Piper Cub, trying to determine if a full-scale salvage project would be economically worthwhile. The plane had munched into the mountain on a blustery January day. The pilot, a veteran Shasta flyer, had last been heard over his radio while 1.5 miles from the mountain on his Redding-to-Medford flight. His frozen body was removed two days after the crash.

Most days, the 56-year-old Corder is a welder at Weyerhauser. Other days he scans mountainous airplane wrecks. A few years ago he salvaged an airtanker that smacked into the hills between Klamath Falls and Ashland. In the 1970s he did the same in the Grand Tetons.

"I don't have any desire to climb the mountain because 'it's there' or because I want my name in a book at the top. I do it because there's a plane wreck."

The hike down the mountain started uneventfully enough. Until fatigue, weariness, and possibly tensions created by jumping over yawning crevasses — and sparse oxygen — overcame his partner. Stops were made every few minutes as day turned to twilight and twilight darkened to night. Above treeline they sighted lights at Horse Camp, the Sierra Club cabin where they'd made camp. But once in the trees, the guiding lights disappeared. They wandered uncertainly.

"You've heard these stories about the mountain," says Corder. "I'm not much a believer about the supernatural, but I'll tell you, we had a helping hand. And it's not our imagination."

Corder and his companion had cached their backpacks. His friend insisted Corder help him build a rock wall, leave him there for the night, and continue on. Corder refused. They struggled on.

"By golly, about 9:30 we saw a flash. It looked like somebody coming through the woods with a flashlight. We thought, boy, this is great. They're going to bring some hot coffee to us or something warm and help us get off this durned mountain."

Suddenly the lights were three. One shone bright, steady, unmoving. The others seemed to pass through the trees. Corder and his friend walked toward the lights. They flashed Corder's light. Two lights flashed back. Corder guesses it took about four minutes from the time they saw the lights, altered their direction toward them, and, while walking, again sighted the lights near Horse Camp.

"As soon as we got far enough to see those bonfire lights at Horse Camp, we never saw them again," says Corder of the unexplained beacons, his fingers unconsciously snapping emphasis. "They were out. It kind of gave us an odd feeling."

At Horse Camp, they visited with the resident lodge carekeeper. Earlier, Corder and his friend had found a sack of avocados, mayonnaise, cheese and tuna fish the caretaker had lost. The trio sipped a cup of burgundy in celebration. The caretaker listened while Corder and his friend detailed their occurrences, then talked of other climbers with similar experiences. And no, the caretaker told them, no search party had been sent.

He offered speculations. How would the lost pair have reacted if a flaming chariot had appeared and its driver offered a ride down the mountain? What if "other people" had appeared and tendered a guiding hand? Or, were flickering flashlights things Corder and his friend — and other mystically-assisted Shasta climbers — could accept and understand?

Corder has been careful about retelling his story. He spurns a "kook" label. Little oddities continue to fester his imagination.

"At the time it wasn't weird or odd, but looking back..."

Corder's unusual night happened two weekends ago. Since then he's returned to Shasta's flanks to retrieve his pack. "I wouldn't hesitate to go back again," he said.

He has been acquainted with a Shasta night.

"...day turned to twilight, and twilight darkened to night..." Mysterious flashing lights directed Don Corder and his hiking companion to the Sierra Club cabin.

photo by Dick Bliss

Chapter 17

Angel Clouds
Converge
Over Mt. Shasta

A shrine

many times enhanced

by strange

lenticular clouds

which forever hover

just above

her snowy peaks

*I*n the late 1970s I interviewed a university student from the east coast who was attending the annual conclave of the St. Germain Foundation. He said he had a story to tell and wished to show me some beautiful photos of clouds in the form of angels.

He had always been a cloud-watcher, he said, and was taking cloud pictures on a summer day in 1978, a day when there were many clouds in the sky. Then he handed me a photo of some exceptionally beautiful clouds and said, "The thought came to me to turn around, which I did. I faced south and saw some clouds drifting toward me from the Dunsmuir area."

At that point he showed me a little card which showed a picture of "star angels," the reproduction of which had been taken from a very old edition of John Milton's *Paradise Lost*.

"I saw this manifestation," he continued, "and I thought to myself 'that looks an awful lot like the star angels on the card' and I sent my love to the Angelic Beings and they crystallized into these very clear, distinct forms. I had the feeling at the time that it was a happy occasion, a joyous greeting — that they were angel beings and they were getting together for a great outpouring over this area."

"Then they drifted on and headed toward Mt. Shasta. And another cloud came in. It looked sort of rectangular. It came up just a small distance from the St. Germain amphitheater site and then stopped moving. After it stopped, it crystallized into these forms of angels." He pointed to the photos I held.

He paused, and then explained, "I had a single lens reflex Minolta camera and I needed a wide-angle lens because the angel clouds just covered the sky. During that period every cloud from miles around, from every possible direction, was heading toward Mt. Shasta. Physically, you can't have wind from every possible direction heading toward one point unless it's going straight up — but you can't have clouds on top of the mountain then. It was beautiful. They kept on moving toward the mountain. And 20 minutes after I had taken that picture there was not a cloud in the sky. They all went to the mountain. I thought it was the most gorgeous thing I had ever seen."

I studied the photograph and others. He was right. The clouds really did look like angelic beings. What I saw in his photos were clouds in the form of angels converging over Mt. Shasta, and then they seemed to descend into the mountain. I knew it was odd to see clouds moving in four directions at one time, but photos do not lie.

"Every single cloud goes to the north or to the south usually," he said, "but not these. You should have seen me. I was running around everywhere trying to find someone with a wide-angle lens."

I asked if I could have copies made and he said he would send me several photos after he returned home. "I feel so privileged," he said, "to have seen this 'happening' — I didn't tell anybody about it until after I had the pictures developed. I was so grateful that I had taken my camera along that day."

Though I am positive his intentions were honorable, I have not received the photographs. But I did see his photographs of the angel clouds converging over Mt. Shasta.

Speaking of lofty peaks and clouds, the local lenticular clouds are very beautiful, too, and they can be seen hovering like a halo over Mt. Shasta. Some say a mysterious halo.

Lenticular clouds are not listed among the ten principal clouds because this lovely disc-shaped cloud is not seen everywhere. As a matter of fact, the formation of these clouds occur only in mountainous areas, especially along the coastal mountains.

According to the local meteorologist, these clouds are called "lenticular" because they are lens-shaped. He said they were caused by strong winds aloft, up and around the mountain. In other words, when warm moist air moves up the side of a hill or over a mountain range, it is lifted and cools by expansion. This cooling causes the water vapor to condense and form clouds that hang over the mountains. Lovely lenticular clouds.

Ah, but there is more. Rumors have always been rampant around mystic Mt. Shasta that spaceships are enveloped in these legendary circles of white — that when the lenticular clouds hover around and over this particular mountain, flying saucers are landing or taking off.

Sometimes a fleet of pure white circular clouds can be seen drifting slowly toward Mt. Shasta, and many times one cloud will cap the mountain for long periods of time — which always gives rise to new speculation about spacecraft activity. Sometimes the unusual clouds hang in there all day, their shapes changing all the time as air funnels in and out continuously.

They float like snowy silver dollars over Mt. Shasta's glistening peak. They seem to fit into the splendor and magnificence of the mountain because these clouds, too, are pristine and pure, and, yes, mysterious. And if you let them, they'll have a hypnotic effect upon you and carry your imagination beyond the utmost realm of human thought.

Lenticular clouds, rumors have always been rampant around mystic Mt. Shasta that space-ships are enveloped in these legendary circles of white.

photo by Bobby Richardson

Chapter 18

Cosmic Lady
Visits Mt. Shasta

We are coming

to an age of great light —

and love," she said softly.

"So I tune in to the

consciousness of marvels

like Solomon, Plato, Socrates,

Moses, Freud, Jung and many other

incredible minds."

Before going into the subject of spaceships seen in the area surrounding Mt. Shasta, it would be well to relate an interview with one of the most colorful ladies I have ever met. She arrived in a flurry of rainbow colors on a sunny September day in 1976, and her purpose was to leave this planet alive — in a spaceship. She said she expected to leave planet Earth without the painful experience of dying. Naturally I dropped whatever I was doing in the newsroom and started taking notes.

She was known, she said, as "Cosmic Lady," and she added, "My name is also Janus Aurah Karmah." Actually, her real name was Janice Aurah Kramer and she was born in Brockton, Massachusetts, in 1930, but in 1973 she had accepted the personality of "Cosmic Lady." Since that time she had dedicated her life to channeling messages sent by "cosmic guides" with whom she was in constant psychic contact. Her guides had directed her to Mt. Shasta.

"Why Mt. Shasta?" I asked.

"Mt. Shasta is a major spaceship station," she said. "Around Shasta are a lot of nonbelievers, which is part of the cosmic paradox, but I am so especially privileged to be here at this very holy place. Who knows, I may get my spaceship pickup here."

"If my guides mean for me to go back to Santa Cruz, I will do more groups. I've had oodles of one-to-one seedplanting — you know, turning the soil. But my first choice is leaving this planet because when Cosmic Lady does the rainbow poof, when she goes through the veil of death without dying, just think how much easier it will be for others who don't want to go out the hard way.

"We are coming to an age of great light — and love," she said softly.

I stared hard at this small, intense lady. She was admittedly 46 years old. She was dressed in rainbow colors, draped with meaningful pendants, and her headcovering was aglow with sparkling stones and colorful feathers. She explained herself as being "naturally me, and that's vast and complex."

After spending hours with her, I would certainly agree that she was vast and complex. She could quote Freud, Spinoza, Plato, Socrates, Jung, and she knew all about I Ching, the Cabbala, and astrology. She taught New Age therapy, and I found myself hanging on to every word. Frankly, sometimes she lost me completely.

I admitted this and she chuckled. "I'm a channel for this particular expression of the gift of love. I ask for divine inspiration and then just open up to receive the flow. Since there is only death of material and physical bodies, in this philosophy, the universe is a giant warehouse of everything that ever was, is, and will be. So I tune in to the consciousness of marvels like Solomon, Plato, Socrates, Moses, Freud and many other incredible minds."

I asked about her background. She was born January 10th, 1930, in Massachusetts, graduated from high school and moved to Boston for training as a lab technician, after which she moved to New York for one year and worked as a medical secretary. She said she suffered a breakdown working out her karma, but recovered and moved to Washington, D.C., in 1954 where she worked for the Democratic National Committee and also in administration on Capitol Hill.

Los Angeles beckoned in 1957 where she worked as a secretary in a mental retardation clinic and, while there, decided to continue her education in the field of social work. She was 29 years old. Working her way through school, she received a B.A. in Psychology (Phi Beta Kappa) which led to a Master's Degree in Social Welfare at the University of Southern California.

As a trainee she was a probation officer in Watts and also worked in Venice, California, where she counseled and helped young Mexican-American girls. Her first official job as a social worker was with the Volunteers of America Family Council in Los Angeles where she worked with families and also in drug counseling. It was during this period of her life that she joined, in 1969, the New Age group "Movement of Inner Spiritual Awareness" and in 1972 she received one of the first revelations of her life. In a book entitled *Aquarian of Jesus the Christ* the comforter (Holy Spirit) is mentioned as "she" — and even at the time of this interview she considered this a most major revelation.

"New Age therapy will be to the New Age what Freud was to the old," she said to me. "I never imagined I would be doing this. I had a good job in Los Angeles. Money and time and all that used to be very important to me. I worked hard for my Master's degree. Then all this happened and everything changed. I've stayed in hundreds of houses for the last two years. Houses, crash pads, churches, and even a shed in Berkeley. I like the symbology of that: staying in a manger.

"I'm known as Janus. Janus is an archetype, medi-type, proto-type. Janus in Roman mythology is the head that looks in all directions. Janus is also a principle — of third-eye, doorways, windows, shadows, light and dark, good and bad, mirrors, beginnings, endings. My middle name 'Aurah' means light in Hebrew — aura around our bodies, the rainbow that some folks see. And I use the last name 'Karmah' — what goes round comes round."

When asked in another interview by reporter Adi Gevins of the Berkeley Barb if she had followers, Cosmic Lady replied: "Those of us who are free spirits don't have to be gurus. We don't have to charge a lot of earth money. When my channels were first opened, I thought people would flock to me. The New Age therapy I was given to teach is so exciting. Then I realized I would have to do it alone. I have had to move alone and fast ever since. Two years ago the Cosmos sent me penniless to Big Sur like the 'Fool' in the Tarot, to walk through death. They told me they would pick me up and take me back home. The Cosmos works in funny ways. I wandered in the hills and waited but they never came."

"I see," I said, not really seeing at all. "This spaceship you're waiting for now, where do you think it will take you?"

"I've been told I leave the planet." she said. "And my consciousness leaves in a rainbow, possibly. I was sent to Mt. Shasta for specific reasons. It's one of the most holy places on the planet, indeed. As to the place I will go, whether we call it the inner realms, heaven, the source, the light — my consciousness leaves and spends three and one-half years, more or less, doing what I've been doing on this level. For one thing, my consciousness channels a wisdom system and planet Earth is in trouble.

"Way back under the aeons," she continued, "the karmaic plot for Earth was devised — this series of millennium beginning with Mu, Atlantis, Egypt, the Inca, the Aztec, the Maya, and so forth — and we, so it goes, 'needed' the crucifixion, the inquisition, Hitler, bombs, Vietnam, a few world wars, so that a spiritual Watergate could take place. We're coming to the junction, the renewal time. There's no judgement day. That would be too simple if a big hand pointed left and right. Because, for one thing, there is no eternal damnation. There is no hell. Earth has been a training planet so this level that I reflect is the level above consciousness-raising. We are pure consciousness.

"There are no 'thems.' We are all 'us'es' and it's a matter of karma. Karma is a state of consciousness, as is everything. America, we had to practice for 200 years. While so many of us, everywhere, are seeing that all over the planet we want the same thing. We are life. We are worth more than money. Consider America. Black's got slavery, Jew's got the road. Especially in America. A hodgepodge brought together. So when we see in terms of the giant cosmic soap-opera, we come here throughout many incarnations to transcend the idiocy and the horror and the ridiculousness of the Earth level."

Her strange rainbow-hued costume fascinated me. Even in today's world of anything-goes, she was unique. I asked her about it.

"My costumes are fun. They express the many dimensions of my personality. I love being eccentric now. It feels right and natural and expresses my complexity," she said, smiling. "Also, I work with color and healing and I love varying expressions of color patterns. My feathered hat is especially joyous to me. It's magic, as is life, and feathers are a symbol of wisdom in many cultures."

She was, she said, finally herself and she had found that life is really a marvelous stage. "I'm an Earthling. But I've transcended. I've paid my dues. I live on pennies and I've slept in a few hundred places during the last few years as Cosmic Lady. I have been treated really shabbily by most folks. Most Christians are not very Christian. Christianity is in very serious trouble. We all work out the 'Christ' and the 'anti-Christ' and if we have judgments, if we waggle our finger at someone and accuse them of the anti-Christ, then we are not learning how to be selfless and ever more humble and loving, as we each must in our time. It feels good to be good."

Cosmic Lady carried with her what she called a carpet bag, 22" x 28" in dimension, containing her wisdom system, the gift of which was, she said, eternal life. She shares the system with those interested. Vast and complex, like the Cosmic Lady herself, the wisdom system consisted of large wisdom wheels of New Age therapy.

"Would you explain your wisdom system?" I asked, eyeing the colorful wheels.

"The wisdom system that I have the privilege of channeling," she explained, "is how to really, with great cosmic awareness and sensitivity, use the divine sciences. For instance, we built the pyramids by levitation, and with third-eye, laser, we put our energies into cutting those big blocks and transporting them across the lands. Look at the pyramid buildings in South America in the very high mountains.

"There is no way that Earth-level slaves could have done most of that.

"The understanding of metaphysics is the thorough knowledge of divine law as it comes in through the sciences. Earth-level scientists are in a lot of trouble with all the genetic experimentations. Look at the method of freezing our bodies for immortality. Why? We are already immortal. So there exists what I call especially wavy lines.

"And take Earth-level justice. In America we are karmically so complacent on so many levels. The 'good old days' were not that good. We went out to manifest destiny and saved, we thought, the world for democracy. The New Age will be a cosmic universal spiritual government with a touch of democracy, a dab of socialism, some communism, all updated, of course. You see, we are coming to a time when we will look very clearly around the planet and see that we are all 'us' — we are all incredible spiritual beings, so in cleansing our closet we revere life.

"Obviously the planet has to be cleansed. And also apparently obvious, there are so many on the planet who, unless great miracles occur in karma, will not be evolved enough to live in a civilized society. So we usually have to do what we call 'die' to renew contracts. On the inner realms there is no such thing as time, we do not have a body, and we may stay on the inner realms for many lifetimes. In the next years we will be given choices: Everyone on the planet will know that if we, indeed, want to stay here, we will be here because we love Mother Earth, because we love each other. And if we want to move on because we're old or sick or tired or finishing ancient incarnational patterns, when we have cleared our 'third eye' and our heart, we won't have to leave in many of the atrocious, horrendous ways of the old consciousness. And if we are not evolved enough yet to really serve the 'Light' and we have to work out more incarnational patterns, then we will choose to leave."

Cosmic Lady paused for a moment. "It takes a while to get used to. Life is such an incredible gift — we walk, we talk, we sing, we dance, we think, we make love, we create. So we are all creators. We are Divinity. And once we know what it is we are here to do, well...like when my consciousness accepted 'Cosmic Lady' there was no way I could not do it the way it came through me.

"Whatever we do, there is always somebody who says do it, don't do it, do it another way, stop it, be normal and our minds have been so full of corruption and greed and confusion and the wondering of 'who am I?' When all the time, up and down throughout the ages, there has been Light. We're it. We are Light. We are Light. We are unioning now our Divinity, whether we call it soul, spirit, life. But we're it. More of us are now consciously surrendering."

I asked her about her "rainbow" image.

"The rainbow is healing and is the mark of God's covenant that he/she/it will not destroy the Earth. This is the butterfly age. Many of us are emerging from the moth stage through the cocoon into universal citizenship. And the sun is the giant battery of solar energy from the one source which we can enter for more love, peace, and light. We are, all of us, everything. Some of us, of course, have more profound orchestrations. My life is dedicated to serving and helping to bring in the New Age through expanded awareness. My consciousness is free spirit, and it serves Mother/Father and tends to reach the most disillusioned, the most disenfranchised, the most damaged flowers."

And you believe," I asked, "that all Earthlings live with this Infinite Invisible — this Omnipresence?"

"Most certainly," she nodded. "On every heartbeat. The small mind of each of us is channeled to the Big Mind."

The interview was over. I followed her to the door and we said goodbye. I walked in the fresh air for awhile, trying to assimilate the complexities of the strange interview. Then an incredible thing happened. There, in a perfect arc over Mt. Shasta, was a rainbow. I have seen many rainbows arc over Mt. Shasta but what puzzled me most about this rainbow was — it hadn't been raining.

I stared at it for a few moments, trying hard to recall one of the last things she had said after the interview: "One of the signs of the coming age of enlightenment will be the rainbow light-show in the sky when Cosmic Lady is returned home."

"Mt. Shasta is a major spaceship station," she said. "Around Shasta are a lot of nonbelievers which is part of the cosmic paradox, but I am so especially privileged to be here at this very holy place — and who knows, I may get my spaceship pickup here."
Photo by Sally Abbe.

photo by Dick Bliss

Chapter 19

Ufo's, Fact Or Fiction In The Realm Of Mt. Shasta?

Many young spiritual groups

camp on Mt. Shasta during the

summer months. In 1976 the

leader of the "All One Family"

group said he believed that

various spaceships from other planets

had been centering their energies

on the mountain.

Mt. Shasta, glistening superstar of all mountains, has always been synonymous with mystery. Its snowy peaks and ridges seem to join the very rim of heaven and it has always been whispered that those who seek shall find not only the mysteries of the ages but also the future within Shasta's snowy glades. Is it any wonder then that sightings of unidentified objects have been reported on its slopes and within its realm?

Consider the village of Happy Camp, for instance, one of the small settlements around the base of the mountain. Surrounded by precipitous, heavily timbered mountains, it lies deep in the rugged Klamath River canyon. Happy Camp — named by California's early gold miners. Today, descendants of those miners and the Karok Indians continue to live there. The area is extremely remote. Oddly enough, spaceships have been sighted there, and residents claim they have been abducted.

When sightings actually occur in the small hamlets surrounding Mt. Shasta, often they are not reported. Or if they are, the persons reporting a sighting often retract everything they say for fear of public ridicule or for fear of losing their jobs, to say nothing of the annoying telephone calls.

It has always been rumored that Mt. Shasta is a fueling station for spacecraft, and that they hide in the strange lenticular clouds which frequently form a perfect halo over the mountain.

And we have already explored in an earlier chapter, Dr. Doreal's theory that the Atlanteans, after engaging in a victorious war with the Lemurians, imprisoned the hapless Lemurians beneath the Caroline Islands in the Pacific and sealed the entrance, establishing an elaborate guard system which prohibits the Lemurians to ever escape their bondage. And according to Doreal, the Atlanteans, who still live in a secret city miles beneath the mountain, still commute by spaceship every three months to that area in the South Pacific.

And so, there are those who believe that some of the spaceships gliding locally on magnetic currents on moonlight nights are Atlanteans and they live inside Mt. Shasta.

Whether or not the general public accepts the reality of spacecraft, the overwhelming fact is they have been sighted too often in the Mt. Shasta area to discount the reality that they exist.

As long ago as October 24, 1955, it was reported that long-time resident W. A. Barr, his wife and their housekeeper observed a brilliant light on the mountain about eight o'clock in the evening. They said the light seemed to revolve in small circles. Barr was quoted as saying "it had every color and glittered like a diamond."

It was about that same time that the late J. O. McKinney (better known as "Mac" around the Mt. Shasta area and one-time feature writer for numerous newspapers and magazines) told me in an interview that he had seen something very exciting and strange while working as nightwatchman at the McCloud River Lumber Company. Making his rounds one night, he had gone up into the watchtower overlooking the McCloud lumber yards. All four walls of the tower were glass.

McKinney said, "Eight or ten 'lights' came swooping toward the tower in formation, very rapidly, with no sound at all. They were white and brilliant and looked as though they were flying 300 to 400 feet above the ground." When his view was cut off by the roof, McKinney rushed over to the other side of the tower, but they never reappeared.

A woman who lives in the suburbs of the city of Mount Shasta, a friend of mine who wishes to remain anonymous, noticed a strange plume-shaped cloud one day about 14 years ago. Directly under the cloud was a disc-shaped spaceship which, she said, had beautiful, iridescent-colored lights and seemed to be hovering about 400 feet above the valley floor. She got into her car and drove closer, finally stopping in at the Pine Grove Grocery nearby to tell Curley Hurlbert, who was the proprietor then. After taking a look, Hurlbert thought at first it was a plane, but decided a plane could not hover in one spot so long, as this object was doing. Then it vanished.

In the late 1960s, a Mount Shasta police officer (who, for obvious reasons also wishes to be nameless) said in an interview with reporter Garth Sanders of the *Redding Record-Searchlight* that he had seen two of the "things." The first time was in the fall of 1963. He and another officer were patrolling during the night in the police car. They noticed lights against the dark bulk of 9,700' Mt. Eddy to the west. At first they thought the lights came from a jeep on one of the many logging roads there, but when they put their field glasses on the object, they saw a disc or "covered saucer" and it had a row of lights along its side.

As usual, it was one of the area's beautiful moon-splashed nights. The officer estimated the length of the disc at 30 to 50 feet and said its ring of lights shifted from brilliant green to red to silver. Then in a burst of speed, it whisked away over Mt. Eddy, which is situated across a valley from Mt. Shasta.

The men notified the United States Air Force and were subsequently mailed stacks of detailed questionnaires. When they finally filled them out, the Air Force decided the two police officers had been mistaken about what they had seen.

A few years later the same officer was alone in the patrol car just north of the city of Mount Shasta. Again there was moonlight. He knew there was something hovering overhead and very close. He leaned forward and looked upward through the patrol car's sloping windshield. He said the spaceship was about 40 feet in diameter, saucer-shaped, and was equipped with a pair of curved skids or pipes on its underside. The craft gave off a brilliant blue light. He radioed the dispatcher at the police station and asked him to go out into the street and see if he could sight the object. The dispatcher did so and immediately returned to the office to report that he had indeed seen a "big blue light." He returned outside to witness the craft hovering for awhile, then abruptly it zipped to the area above the St. Germain Foundation's amphitheater on upper McCloud Avenue (in the city of Mount Shasta). Again it hovered, drifting slightly. Then it skimmed eastward and disappeared over one of the highest ridges of Mt. Shasta.

Then, of course, there were the Happy Camp sightings. In November, 1975, unearthly "occurrences" were getting the natives a little excited in and around that isolated hamlet which is neatly tucked away in a colorful blend of narrow valleys, steep forested mountains, rocky cliffs, and the Klamath River.

It seems that five Happy Campers had gone into the hills above the town one night to investigate the source of bright lights seen the night before. While there, they reportedly heard strange electronic sounds and saw bright lights flashing. Then a flying saucer appeared. They not only yelled at it but fired their automatic weapons for several rounds. There was no response, but three of them felt as though their lungs had turned to stone, and they had great difficulty breathing.

After much local consideration, it was finally decided that the happening was probably a Caltrans survey crew who had been bouncing lights off the mountain while surveying it.

However, Gary Mortenson, publisher of the esteemed *Pioneer Press* newspaper in nearby Fort Jones, interviewed the five men and discovered that on the night of November 23rd, two of the men were using a citizen's band radio on Shinar Ridge when a bright red, moon-sized object came hurtling toward their car, then veered away. Going immediately over to the spot where it had happened, they found little piles of vermiculite and tripod-like impressions in the ground.

Returning two nights later to show a friend, they reportedly heard two tones so eerie that they trained a highpowered spotlight at the vicinity from which the chilling sounds emanated and looked into a pair of silver-blue, wide-set eyes that seemed, one of them said, to "drink up all the light." So they left and returned with two more men. They all claim to have seen some manlike figures moving about in the bushes and one of the Happy Camp men fired several rounds into the night air. Once again, three of the five had trouble breathing. They decided to get out of that area and retreated down the mountain with what they described as a "big light" at their heels.

But the biggest news to come out of Happy Camp was a "close encounter of the third kind." A little research explained the different types of encounters. Sighting a UFO is an encounter of the first kind. If the UFO leaves behind physical evidence or causes physical evidence (electrical interference, for instance), it is an encounter of the second kind. A close encounter of the third kind is when the observer has contact with "beings" on the craft, and just eye contact will do.

In the November 14, 1979, issue of the Fort Jones *Pioneer Press*, reporter Hazel Davis writes of Happy Camp's Helen White, who had appeared during a segment of *Real People* viewed on national television on Wednesday of the previous week. White was one of the three persons interviewed during the MUFON (Mutual Unidentified Flying Object Network) UFO Convention held in Burlingame, California, for three days in July, 1979.

Helen White claimed to have been abducted by unidentified "beings" manning the spacecraft. During the television presentation on *Real People*, the interviewer explained that all three of the women were put under hypnosis to tell of their happenings, and, in listening to them, he had been "impressed" by facts revealed in the sessions.

White told of being abducted along with two men from Happy Camp who had trap lines on Cade Mountain. The men, White said, went to a clearing there, away from town, to shoot their guns. Her first abduction (with the two men) in November, 1976, occurred on Cade Mountain. A strange ship landed and two "beings" emerged from the craft. White said there were other residents present, but they experienced a choking sensation and left before she and the men were abducted.

She remembered that "everything lit up" and one of the locked doors of their car opened. From that point they could remember nothing until later, when they awoke in the sky aboard the craft. The beings spoke English and the trio was assured that they would not be hurt. And later, when they were returned and released, they still didn't seem to know what happened. She did remember being back in the automobile, driving home and singing "There is Power in the Blood," an old religious hymn.

Then in late 1978, she was in the same area cutting wood with her young grandson. Again a spacecraft landed near them and the beings rendered her grandson unconscious by means of some weird device. White thought they had killed him and cried, whereupon one of the beings told her the child was not hurt and not to be afraid. She and her grandson were taken aboard the craft, she was examined, and then they were allowed to return to earth.

In September, 1979, White was again cutting wood in the Mill Creek area when she had another encounter of the third kind. She had just cut up a log and had started splitting the wood when she was tapped on the shoulder by another being. This time she ran to her pickup and drove down the mountain as fast possible. When she got home, she found black and blue marks on her arms and shoulders.

Helen White also reported sighting spacecraft from the window of her home in Happy Camp, and claims the beings have also visited her at her home. At one time one of them was standing in her bedroom. She said the beings are very intelligent, they knew what she was thinking, and when she asked them where they came from, they said she wouldn't understand because she did not understand the universe.

Other sightings occurred during the same time:

July 14, 1979: A well-known Dunsmuir couple were driving northward towards Tulelake, California, on Highway 139. The countryside was cast in darkness on this moonless night, and, as the camper pickup drove along, its headlights provided the only source of illumination for miles around. Suddenly an intense white light bathed the camper with its glow, and then it appeared, a green and gold torpedo-shaped object with a rounded front. It was flying north by northwest. The object was only 300 yards from the camper and looked to be the size of a 40-foot housetrailer. The object first appeared in the sky but came down gracefully, paralleled the road and the camper, then went down the road and out of sight.

Harry Drew, director of the Klamath Falls County Museum in nearby southern Oregon, also saw what he described as a green and gold object that same night about 10:56 p.m., just seconds after the Dunsmuir couple sighted the craft. He said it was extremely visible and very large, about the size of an automobile.

October, 1979: Three sightings of a "bright, white light in the sky" were reported to the Siskiyou County sheriff's office in Yreka, California. According to an eye witness, he was walking his dog at approximately 11 p.m. on a Thursday night when he saw the object. He said the night was pitch black, but the illumination from the object "lit up the surroundings"; it was traveling northward, at approximately 1,000 feet in elevation. When the object dropped to eye level, it began to turn orange, then went completely dark. That same night, two Crescent City, California, policemen reported spotting an unidentified flying object at approximately the same time. It was green in color, and one of them said he viewed the object for about 15 seconds before it disappeared. Other sightings on the same night were reported by a Smith River woman, a man in Humboldt County, and a person in Klamath Falls, Oregon.

January 6, 1980: While Dorris, California, may not be known on a national map, it may be better known on celestial maps. At least one long-time Dorris resident thinks so. He has a story to tell, but wishes to remain anonymous. While returning to Dorris from Klamath Falls, Oregon, on January 6, 1980, he was followed and "observed" by what he described as a giant, brightly illuminated spaceship. He first observed the craft between Kingsley Field and Highway 97 just out of Klamath Falls.

He decided to stop his car and watch it, but when he stopped, it stopped. When he moved, it moved exactly at his speed. Once it rushed up on him from behind. He was watching in his rear-view mirror, but just when he thought it was going to hit his car, it nosed up, flew over his truck, went off to the side, then flew alongside him.

He said it was about 35–40 feet across and perfectly round. The light from it was so bright he couldn't make out any detail on it at all. It lit up, he said, everything around him.

The craft followed him all the way to Dorris Hill, flying about house-top high off the ground all the time. It was so foggy, he became concerned that it would crash into the hill. But then he didn't see it anymore. It had vanished as suddenly as it had appeared.

September, 1980: Two families were weekend-houseboating on Trinity Lake. It was after 10 p.m. when they spotted something in the sky over Lewiston, California. They thought it was a satellite, but then it was joined by another object. The two began moving strangely. They would move, stop, move, stop, and they looked like they were flying in formation. They were reportedly large, yellow objects. Moving northwest over Trinity Lake, they suddenly accelerated to a terrific speed and disappeared.

October, 1980: A Weed, California, police officer dubbed the sighting as a "close encounter of the worst kind." He said it looked like a bright star over the southern shoulder of Mt. Shasta. The Weed police reported receiving several calls from residents who watched the same object about 5 o'clock in the morning.

November, 1980: Redding, California, police received several reports of strange lights in the sky in what apparently was a mass sighting of UFOs in northern California. Officials at the Federal Aviation Administration tower in nearby Red Bluff said the Shasta County sheriff's office called saying several persons had reported seeing orange, red, and white lights in the sky. The FAA said the lights were reported throughout northern California and were seen by several airplane pilots. They were described as being in groups of three red-and-orange glowing balls that left vapor trails in their wake. The lights were reported during a four-hour period. One resident said she was driving on Highway 44 about 7 p.m. when she saw two big, bright white lights. They left vapor trails behind them, followed by six to eight more vapor trails without lights. It was, she said, just beautiful. She got out of her car and called for them to come back.

November, 1980: From the November 24, 1980, issue of the Yreka-based *Siskiyou Daily News*.

UFO Investigator Paul C. Cerny of Mountain View took time out from a fishing trip on the Klamath River to check into recent reports of UFO sightings in the area. Cerny, a mechanical engineer who has spent 24 years investigating UFO phenomena, is no stranger to the area. He has traveled here before to interview persons in the Happy Camp and Mount Shasta area who claim to have observed out-of-this-world space-ships.

Cerny said, "I know the freeway like the back of my hand I've been up here so many times." He talked with a resident of Yreka who was among those who had seen two lights streaking across the sky on a clear night. He said he and a friend were walking down Butte Street about 8 o'clock in the evening when they watched the lights gradually cruise along toward Paradise Craggy. Then one of the lights disappeared. They watched the other one for 10 or 15 seconds, then it disappeared. The lights had been traveling at the same speed of an airplane but were definitely not the running lights of an aircraft. These objects were noiseless at an estimated distance of about 1,000 feet.

Others reported the sighting. Some called from McCloud, another small town on the slopes of Mt. Shasta. Another call came from Beaver Creek (Klamath River area) from a lady who said she was in her auto waiting to pick up her husband about two miles from Horse Creek when the lights appeared. She said the bright lights were the color of a light-bulb and were heading northeast. But she said they came straight at her auto and "floated around" before disappearing.

Cerny recounted a sighting he experienced in February, 1976, in Happy Camp with another investigator and a local resident. They were, he said, on a ridge when they saw an orange glow coming from a rectangular-shaped object. He said it was like looking at the sun.

Cerny could not explain why he and the others did not drive to the object, which was less than a mile away, for further investigation. Instead, the trio left the area. He said they felt they were mind-manipulated not to come near it. This sighting came during that period from November, 1975 to April, 1976 when there were continuous sightings in the Happy Camp area, and he has talked to the three persons who claim they were taken aboard the craft. He stated that it is typical for people who claim they were abducted by aliens to also have their mind wiped clean of the experience, and it oftentimes takes hypnosis to discover clues to what actually happened.

Some experts do not think these objects represent extraterrestrial spaceships, but they do suggest that they certainly represent phenomena that lie outside the present structure of science. In September, 1976, when it became known that I was working on a newspaper feature concerning spacecraft, I received through the mail (anonymously) several interesting publications which print channeled messages (channeled to certain illuminated persons in the city of Mount Shasta and other places) from a spacebeing named MONKA, who allegedly is the protector of our planet known as Earth.

According to the publication, MONKA once lived on Earth as "Viracocha" who was an Inca leader in Peru, and was, at that time, representative of the Space

Confederation as Protector of the Earth Planet. Other spacebeings who were reportedly being channeled regularly in 1976, were HATONN and SOLTEC. HATONN was allegedly the record-keeper for the galaxy and this part of the universe. He predicted (then) that we were upon the threshold of a new breakthrough in understanding and cooperation.

SOLTEC, on the other hand, was a sun technician. He was hoping to find ways and means whereby spacebeings could mingle with Earth people as one great civilization. SOLTEC was quoted as saying that Earth people must raise their consciousness and join the peoples of higher dimensions.

On a channeling received dated February 18, 1976, MONKA is reported to have said: "We of the space world have much activity surrounding Mt. Shasta and that territory. We do have activities going on there at this time. You have heard of many sightings of our ships and the phenomena which appear in the heavens over Mt. Shasta and around it. And you have even seen pictures of likenesses of our ships. They seem to be formed in the clouds. Some of them are clouds but it is designed that you, the ones who are looking and hoping to see us, are to have hope and courage and to know that we are there. We are real.

"MONKA explained that many things were preserved in Mt. Shasta before the cataclysm of the continent (it is assumed he was referring to Lemuria). He said the mountain was used to preserve the "precious flames" and many of the records which were kept and preserved and did not go down with the continent. He added that they are there now and shall always be kept safely from any "outer darkness."

According the the publication, another spacebeing known as NETTONE "channeled" to a person in New Mexico the following: "Our spaceship, the "Lanastria" traverses planet Earth many times. Recently we have noted that there is more spiritual light emanating from the Earth than ever before. Today mankind on Earth faces confusion because he experiences great insecurity. He does not know how to take care of himself, he does not know where to go or what to do. Although he mentally accepts a greater power he calls God, he has not the faith or confidence to turn to that One and ask for help.

NETTONE continued, "Our official mission in this space program is to traverse the earth, sensing and monitoring all segments thereof, taking note of all vibrational changes, and observing man and his doings as closely as possible. Certain of your climactic conditions are caused by outside influences, such as holes in the protective sheath of atmosphere around your planet which permit harmful sun rays to come through to your surface. These holes in the protective layer around the earth are largely caused by bomb-blast activity. These explosions send out radioactive particles which, although invisible, create havoc in the belt of security which should completely surround planet Earth. This testing of bombs must be stopped or mankind on Earth will suffer from and be consumed by a kind of heat he never thought existed. We think, we talk, and we watch mankind, hoping that he will soon realize that he has friends above him and around him, even on his own planet."

In June of 1976, MONKA allegedly stated in one of his channelings that spacebeings are a special, different type of people, and they are waiting for the time when all will be "one brotherhood" but that this would apparently take more time. And he said,

"Be drawn together in brotherhood and love. This is what we desire. If you will but stop to realize, our Great Supreme Divine Creator did not just create one little Earth planet. He has many planets, many worlds, without end, without number. Worlds inhabited. This you will find on the scrolls of antiquity, in the recorded history of the world. These civilizations are far, far ahead of the one which you do now enjoy upon Earth, so this is why we feel it is necessary for us to come to you."

And he added: "Your government does know there are extraterrestrial beings. Your government and your scientists are working today. They are planning. It will be sooner than any of you can believe — this will all come out into the open and you will have this knowledge. You will learn more about the space world."

Many young spiritual groups camp on Mt. Shasta during the summer months. In 1976 the leader of the "All One Family" group said he believed that various spaceships from other planets had been centering their energies on the mountain.

He agreed that out in space a confederation exists and he said that they are trying to raise Earth to a higher energy level so that they can contact this planet. According to him, planet Earth is considered to be on a low level.

He stated in an interview that another planet is being readied for Earthlings who have succumbed so completely to materialism that they have not become aware of, and therefore have been unable or unwilling to accept the fact that soon the cosmos must move into the higher cycle. Those errant Earthlings will be taken off Earth for another cycle on another planet to develop and elevate their consciousness, however long it takes. Earth, he said, has the smallest part in a cosmic cycle of change. Caught up in materialism, man is unable anymore to survive the coming baptism by fire that will end the Piscean Age. And by the year 2000, the cosmos must move into the higher cycle, the Aquarian Age.

The Piscean Age, he explained, was one of separation, people doing their own trips. In the Aquarian Age, people will maintain their individuality but become a total part of the group.

Strangely enough, whatever the UFO phenomenon is, it comes and goes unexpectedly. The decade of the 1980s was unusually lacking in spacecraft sightings in and around Mt. Shasta. Could it be possible that space beings are handling their observations in such a manner that we are no longer aware of them? Or have they decided that we on Earth are not capable of living as they probably do on other planets where war has most certainly been eliminated, along with poverty, intolerance, racial bias, disease, bombs and crime?

photo courtesy Neil & Carl Clement

Chapter 20

Was Mu The Cradle Of Civilization?

The members of the

Lemurian Fellowship

reportedly believe that everyone

living on earth

today is a

descendant of the

world's original civilization,

Mu.

Near San Diego and situated high on a mountain is the headquarters of an international group that claims its origin to the lost continent of Mu (also known as Lemuria).

The "Lemurian Fellowship" is a mystery cult, an esoteric philosophical society, and according to Reynolds G. Dennis, head of the fellowship, "We live in accord with laws laid down 78,000 years ago during the prime of the greatest civilization the world has ever known."

Charles Hillinger, *Los Angeles Times* staff writer, has been tracking down Lemurian stories for years (he has interviewed many residents of Mount Shasta) and so it was inevitable that he would discover the Lemurian Fellowship. His piece, datelined July 31, 1977, included an interview with Reynolds Dennis who was 67 at the time.

According to Dennis, Mu was seven times larger than North America. It covered most of the Pacific Ocean and included Australia, New Zealand, the Philippines, Hawaii, the Aleutians, southwestern Alaska, the west coasts of Canada and the United States, Baja, California, and hundreds of other islands.

Dennis also said that the world has always been three-quarters water and one-quarter land, but many of the land masses of today were under water before Mu submerged 25,000 years ago. And when Mu submerged, Atlantis appeared. When Atlantis vanished, the continents we know today were formed in their present configurations.

The Lemurian Fellowship has members scattered throughout the world, but it was not founded until 1936. They believe that the history of the lost continent of Mu and the teachings of the leaders of Mu were revealed to the late Robert D. Stelle, a Chicago homeopathic doctor who founded the fellowship. Stelle headed the group until his death in 1952, when Reynold G. Dennis became president of the board of governors of the Lemurian Fellowship.

The members of the Lemurian Fellowship reportedly believe that everyone living on earth today is a descendant of the world's original civilization, Mu. They believe each and every human being alive today has walked the face of the earth for thousands of years in a succession of different bodies. They believe we have all lived on earth since the very beginning.

Robert Stelle wrote a 436-page book, *The Sun Rises* and it purportedly is the true account of events which occurred 78,000 years ago, the beginning of mankind on earth.

The ultramodern complex of the Lemurian Fellowship on a 60-acre mountain reached by a winding narrow road, includes residential quarters, a headquarters building plus other structures, all set in beautiful park-like surroundings. (Under a huge

"Lemurian Fellowship" sign is another warning "No Visitors.") They also own a hilltop site not far away called "Gateway" on which resides the fellowship's one industry, the manufacture of a large variety of custom-crafted mosaic and terrazzo inlay gifts which are sold in some of the nation's most exclusive shops. Those members who create the gift items live at Gateway and devote their lives to the fellowship. They also correspond with students who live all over the world, students who are in various stages of learning. (Members pay for a series of 12 introductory lessons and each lesson consists of more than 40,000 words. According to Dennis, it takes at least two and a half years to complete the introductory course and many would-be student eventually drop out.)

But other members say their life on the California mountain is peaceful and is a life spent learning more and more about the Mukulian civilization of the lost continent of Mu. The fellowship has detailed maps of Mu and they are complete with names of mountains and valleys. The maps also show the location of the continent's capital, Hamukulia.

The Lemurian Fellowship contends that numerous mysterious relics of Mu have been found on islands throughout the Pacific. Dennis, during his interview with Charles Hillinger, said, "Huge strange symbols hand-hewn in 40-ton monoliths in Fiji are from the lost world of Mu, and so are the mysterious megaliths, the great burial platforms known as ahus, and the huge carved heads of Easter Island.

The members believe that individuals in one life may achieve greatness in one field, and then reappear in another life in a completely different, uninspired career. Different careers, it is believed, round out an individual's eternal ego.

As for the current population explosion, members of the Lemurian Fellowship are not concerned. They reportedly maintain that the Lord Masters and Elders of Mu have revealed (through the Lemurian Fellowship) that there are a total of 13 billion egos in existence and since the world's population is roughly four billion, there are currently not enough bodies for the egos to occupy. Once a world population of 13 billion is reached, they believe, it will not grow larger.

Such is the wisdom of Mu.

Ever so often a new story materializes and the Lemurian legend, it seems, will never vanish into obscurity. Photo by Jim Kottinger

photo by Carl & Neil Clement

Chapter 21

There Is A Mystique About This Mountain...

Businessmen, residents, ranchers,

he said,

all spoke freely of the

Lemurians and their community.

Some told of

rituals at sunset,

midnight,

and dawn.

*T*here is a mystique about Mt. Shasta, rising ethereally white above the green Sacramento Valley, a mystique that stirs the spirit and the imagination of humans far and near.

A California writer named Billie Harshberger wrote in Eureka's *Humboldt Standard* in May, 1936:

"Somewhere in the hidden reaches of western mountains, so the story goes, a strange race of people lives, works and plays — a race of Lemurians who came to these shores from the lost continent of the Pacific.

"An old fanciful tale, you say? Well, that's not the half of it, for there have been stories about these Lemurians from credible witnesses who insist the Lemurians have the power of invisibility.

"Weird lights that flash from Mt. Shasta and queer undecipherable hieroglyphics chiseled in solid rock lend credence to the belief that this race exists. Scientists have puzzled over the possibility that a great continent once reared itself in mid-Pacific islands. Could not the inhabitants have escaped to our shores? I sought out old seamen and they said it was so. I sought old records, logs, and rare writings and they agree. From the lips of weatherbeaten men with eyes trained on far horizons I heard of ancient cultured lands submerged by catastrophe."

Harshberger goes on to say that historians have reported the fact that in California there is evidence to show that people (presumably Lemurians) have lived and taken refuge in the center of an extinct volcano, hidden from all possible worldly observation, and that it is possible that these people of Mt. Shasta are still living. This may explain the invisible city.

Referring to the "lost continent," Harshberger stated there were hundreds of records, geological and historical, to prove that islands have been disappearing and reappearing, sinking and rising in the Pacific since the known world has been recording such happenings. "At Ponape, in the Caroline Islands, 2,300 miles from Japan, is a deserted city known as Metalanim, the ruins of which cover eleven square miles. There are massive walls and great temples which are intersected by miles of artificial waterways. Sailors call it the 'Venice of the Pacific' and Professor Macmillan Brown, an authority on such matters, believes that this could have been built by tens of thousands of laborers. Yet now the place is not large enough to accommodate 20,000 and on all the islands within a radius of 1,500 miles, there are not 50,000 people living today. What happened to all the others?"

Harshberger ends the piece by stating, "Scientists believe that there was once a continent which formerly filled a large part of the world's most extensive maritime basin — the Pacific Ocean. The former home of early Lemurians, I'd say, the last of whom live quietly and pray in Mt. Shasta."

Earlier that same year, in January, John B. Scott wrote a piece for the *Rosicrucian Magazine* in which he told of his trip to investigate Mt. Shasta, saying that the first thing he wished to find out about were the weird lights that had been seen by travelers, and even by astronomers in distant observatories.

"It appears," he observed, "that there is actually a basis for the stories concerning the lights — this is not coupled with the Lemurians, however."

Scott met a person who had spent fifteen years on and around Mt. Shasta. He explained that there are unusual mineral deposits and peculiar physical formations which produce these uncanny effects. Not only that, but combined with certain air currents, even ghostly sounds are produced. And this is not, he said, something incident to Mt. Shasta alone. He gave the example of the traveler on the Rhine listening to the echoes of a pistol shot or two which multiply into machine-gun fire because of the physical formation at a certain point on the river.

He added that there have been and always will be strange lights at certain times on Mt. Shasta though they would not be seen as much in the future as they had been in the past, for good reasons: The government had been doing much work and the nature of this work would, to a certain extent, reduce the phenomena since the latter is concerned with purely physical (or mostly physical) conditions. (The reason he said "mostly" was because he felt the average reader does not consider the ethers as being physical since he cannot see them and knows nothing of them.)

Scott therefore attributed the strange lights on Mt. Shasta to be a combination of moonlight, snow, trees, ether, phosphorus and other minerals, and water. And after exploring the so-called strange sounds on the mountain and the other phenomena, Scott came to the conclusion that there are no Lemurians on or in the mountain. There are no Lemurian temples, and there are no storekeepers who exchanged merchandise for gold nuggets with any strange inhabitants on the mountain.

Then, surprisingly, he wrote that he believed an ancient people still live on Mt. Shasta and that their dwellings or temples are located in inaccessible points on the mountain. He believed that they could be contacted under the right conditions by the right persons, but these ancients are not on the physical plane, nor are their temples.

He concluded by stating he, and others, thought that many earthbound spirits from an old civilization which once existed on the mountain are still there, held closely bound to the earth for centuries by their materialistic natures. Mt. Shasta, he said, seemed to be a "sensitive spot," meaning it is easier to contact those on other planes than in most other places.

Many seeking inspiration or new experiences as well as students of occultism visit the mountain during all seasons of the year. Mt. Shasta is listed among the seven mountains of mystery. The others are Mt. Ararat in the Caucasus; Mt. Whitney in the Sierra; The Grand Teton (Mt. Gannett) in Wyoming; Mt. Meru in the Andes; Mt. Ruvengari in Africa; Mt. Everest (Shegatsee) in the Himalayas and Mt. Monserat in Spain.

In 1932 a Los Angeles writer, Edward Lancer, was making a business trip to Portland, Oregon, aboard the Shasta Limited a train long since recalled from service. The train, snaking through the torturous Sacramento River Canyon between Redding and Dunsmuir in northern California, passed into open area about five o'clock in the morning.

Lancer couldn't sleep so he went to the observation car and immediately noticed the southern area of Mt. Shasta because a reddish-green light kept flaring up, then fading, then becoming extremely brilliant. His first thought was that it must have been a forest fire, but there was no smoke.

He later said the glow resembled that of Roman candles. Then the rising sun dimmed the light and the train sped northward out of sight of the phenomenon. He was so impressed he felt unable at first to discuss the sight with anyone he had seen. However, when his fellow traveler joined him for breakfast, he asked Lancer, "Did you see the forest fire?"

Lancer quickly asked, "Did you see any smoke?"

When his friend admitted he had not, that he had seen an odd, reddish glow, Lancer was convinced they had seen a mirage.

When the conductor came by, he asked what the mysterious lights were. The conductor said, "The Lemurians, they hold ceremonials up there."

Upon his return from Portland, he decided to tarry awhile in the vicinity of Mt. Shasta to satisfy his curiosity. He rented an automobile and visited three towns at the foot of Mt. Shasta, Mount Shasta, McCloud, and Weed. It was reportedly in Weed that Lancer learned of the "mystic" village inside the mountain. It seemed to be an accepted fact. Businessmen, residents, ranchers, he said, all spoke freely of the Lemurians and their community. Some told of rituals at sunset, midnight, and dawn. They also told him he would never get near the place, that no one was ever able to penetrate the sanctuary.

He was told Lemurians had a power to blend with the scenery if a stranger came too near, and that powers that seem supernatural to us were common on the ancient continent of Lemuria. To illustrate their powers came the story of a forest fire sweeping up Mt. Shasta in the 1930s which was suddenly and mysteriously stopped by unknown forces.

What seemed incredible to Edward Lancer was that the vanished race had been so successful in secreting their identity in a state filled with tourists that their sacred territory remained a mystery to everyone.

In a very old *Overland Monthly* (1908) there appeared a piece dealing with "A Fragment of the Ancient Continent of Lemuria" which stated, "California was a center of a civilization that antedates the continent of Atlantis by thousands of years."

And in Tokyo, Japan, an article released by *The Sun* in 1961 suggested that the continent of Lemuria {Mu) might rise again. A group of Japanese claimed that Mu was the cradle of civilization and it included Christianity, the Maya civilization, and the Incas of Peru. They stated the continent was as large as North and South America combined and that the natives had advanced navigational techniques which enabled them to visit colonies in Egypt, India, Tibet, Japan, and other far-flung places.

In a 1933 issue of the *Kansas City Times* a report was published about a British anthropologist who claimed he had very definite information, plus maps and photographs, regarding a mysterious lost continent buried beneath the waters of the Pacific Ocean.

Was there, indeed, such a continent?

Consider Madagascar, located in the Indian Ocean and one of the largest islands in the world. According to the *Encyclopaedia Brittanica*, "Madagascar was probably joined to Africa, possibly in Triassic times, thus forming part of the Gondwana continent; but the splitting off is very ancient and bordering islands, such as the Seychelles, etc., allow the conclusion that the island belonged to a continent called by geologists "Lemuria" which stretched as far as India, the sinking of which brought about the disappearance of this continent and gave rise to violent volcanic eruptions."

Many believe the Lemurian colonization program extended to other ancient traces of civilizations found in the world today, such as Easter Island and Stone Henge, whose prehistoric stone monuments have never been adequately explained. And could the Lemurians be responsible for the recently discovered lost cities of the Amazon, ancient cities of white stone hidden for centuries in dense, emerald jungles, cities which predated the Incas?

Chapter 22

Local Mystics,
Spiritualists,
Tibetan Lamas,
Zen Buddhists

"One day I opened a book. There

was the Sanskrit work 'Sishta' and

it meant 'great sages of a previous age

who become the seed of the coming

humanity' — and also, the word

'Shasta' in Sanskrit, which means

'teacher'."

Needless to say, reporters and magazine writers frequently visit Mt. Shasta, often taking back with them tongue-in-cheek pieces not only about California's mystery mountain but also about the mystics, metaphysicians, and mediums at its base.

On a July day in 1973, a writer from *Newsweek* interviewed me; he had been told I had written much on the mountain. He said he had come to investigate the mysteries of Mt. Shasta and to delve into the lives of some of the various spiritualists and mystics who live on the lower slopes of Mt. Shasta. He had been in the city of Mount Shasta for days interviewing others, and then spent most of an afternoon at my home trying (it seemed to me) to separate fact from fiction,

The following appeared several weeks later in *Newsweek*:

"Deep in the bowels of northern California's glacier-topped Mt. Shasta lives a race of people known as Lemurians, who are tall and regal and have a third eye in the middle of their foreheads. Or perhaps the mountain folk are survivors of Atlantis, who conquered the Lemurians in battle and have now taken over. Then again, Mt. Shasta may be inhabited by Yaktavians, who have hollowed out the inside of the mountain by the vibration of giant bells and have even generated light for their underground cities by tinkling the bells against atoms of ether. Of course no one has ever seen a Yaktavian because the ultra-high-frequency tolling of a warning bell on the northwest slope of the mountain frightens snoopers away."

In two columns he mentioned briefly several of the religious sects such as the Saint Germain Foundation founded by Guy Ballard, The Radiant School of Seekers and Servers founded by Nola Van Valer, and the Association Sananda and Sanat Kumara. He mentioned Peter Mt. Shasta, and he mentioned the Zen Buddhists, who have no spiritual connection with Mt. Shasta. (Actually, Abbess Jiyu Kennet was so taken by the beauty of Mt. Shasta that she transplanted, several decades ago, her San Franciscan-based Zen Mission Society to a rustically beautiful 15-acre setting just outside the city of Mount Shasta where they live quietly and unobtrusively.)

It would be well, at this point, to tell about my interview with Peter Mt. Shasta; to tell about the Association Sananda and Sanat Kumara headed by Sister Thedra; and to tell about a certain Tibetan lama. The Saint Germain Foundation, more familiarly known locally as the "I Am" sect (the name is derived from Yahweh, the Hebrew word denoting God) was covered in a previous chapter of this book, as was Nola Van Valer's Radiant School of Seekers and Servers.

I interviewed Peter Mt. Shasta in November of 1973 mostly because I wondered about his name.

"Why did you change your name to Peter Mt. Shasta?" I asked this gentle doe-eyed young man.

"Two years ago," he explained, "I was camping on the mountain. I had just returned from India. I knew nothing about the mountain at that time, I was just camping up there. I awoke at six o'clock one morning and heard a voice saying, 'This is the New Age and you have been born anew. Your name is 'Mt. Shasta' and I said 'Peter Mt. Shasta?' and the voice said, 'Yes, Peter Mt. Shasta.'"

"I still didn't take it too seriously," he continued, "but I thought — it's true, it is a New Age and I do feel as though I've been reborn. My experience in India was such that people who saw me after I returned hardly recognized me, I had changed so much. So I used 'Peter Mt. Shasta' as a pen name and used my other name for business."

Born Peter Anhalt Kraus in Germantown, New York, he had been to India several times, spent some time in Mexico working on a novel, lived in a New York slum area, and had just recently returned from a jaunt to Europe.

Brought up Presbyterian, Peter said, "I think I've been through every path of yoga, every 'ism', and every discipline."

"How did you find out about Mt. Shasta?" I asked.

"In India. An American told me about Mt. Shasta."

"Why did you go to India?"

Peter paused a moment. "I was just awakening to this 'search for the truth' in New York City on the lower east side, a slum neighborhood. I had just come back from Mexico and was working on a novel. After India, I burned it."

I asked him what he did in India.

"The first time I went I really didn't know why I was going. I went to the Himalayas and along the Ganges. The second time I went to southern India, I went back to visit Satya Sai Baba who has a following of millions in India. I have seen him materialize objects."

"Is he a yogi?"

"Well, not in the sense that you would think of a yogi sitting up on a mountain meditating. He's a Master. He called me to come to India to see him. He told me to just meditate on my own God-self. That was the lesson. He said, 'Don't look to me for the answer, look to your own self.' I was just so overwhelmed by him as a person, by the tremendous love coming from him that I wanted to be with him. But he said, 'Don't look to me for that love, it's all within you.'"

"We all looked, in the last age," he continued, "to someone else to give us the answer. In this New Age we're discovering it's all within us."

"Now that you've been to India twice, do you think it's necessary to go to India?"

"No," he said, shaking his head. "Absolutely not. That's one of the points, I think, that will come across in the book I'm writing. I feel it is typical of the search of many young people who are going to India looking for an answer of some kind. As you know, Mt. Shasta attracts all kinds of people. I feel that this is a very special place and there is something very special happening here."

"Like what? What exactly is happening here?"

"I think Mt. Shasta is the focus for building the New Age."

"Do you think Mt. Shasta is a central point of power?"

"Definitely," he answered. "What I find happening here is more exciting than what's happening in India. In India there are amazing people, people who can do amazing things, but as far as the country as a whole, it's falling apart. But in spite of the fact that there's so much chaos and so much hunger, there are an amazing number of happy people there, people who have learned to be happy with nothing."

I asked him about the reported appearance of the Ascended Masters on Mt. Shasta in the 1930s. He said there was a particular reason for making appearances then. Now they try to avoid any type of phenomena, but they are here now just as tangibly as they were then. "They're working more subtly, they don't need to take on bodies in order to work with us so we're going to have to tune into them, to learn how to work with them."

Then he said, "There is a 'city of light' over Mt. Shasta and people seem to be waiting for this city to descend so they can start living in it."

"City of light?" I asked.

"Yes, There is a city of light on a higher plane someplace over this area. We have to build it, that's the whole thing. The city of light is there but we're the ones who have to build it. I think that's the most exciting thing that's happening around here. People are becoming aware."

I closed my notebook. The interview was over. But I was curious about one more thing. "In your opinion, what does the name 'Shasta' mean?" I asked.

Peter Mt. Shasta said reflectively, "I asked to be shown. One day I opened a book. Opened it right to the page. There was the Sanskrit word 'Sishta' and it meant 'great sages of a previous age who become the seed of the coming humanity,' and also, the word 'Shastra' in Sanskrit, which means 'teacher.'"

From a brochure I received some years ago entitled: *Teachings from the Temple of Sananda and Sanat Kumara* came the following:

"This will introduce you to the teachings of the White Brotherhood through the Association Sananda and Sanat Kumara. Mount Shasta, California, is the world headquarters for the Association and located here is the 'Outer Priory' or 'Gate House' of the Monastery of the Seven Rays. Yet the Monastery of the Seven Rays is in Peru, South America, hidden from the outside world in the high Andes near Lake Titicaca.

"After many years of preparation, culminating in five years of intensive training in the Andes, one who is known as Sister Thedra was directed to return to the United States and from there to send forth the teaching of the School of the Seven Rays and the School of Melchezedek. Part of the work of the White Brotherhood, the Spiritual Hierarchy and the Great and Mighty Council, is manifested through these schools.

"By Divine direction, this Association was established to serve as a channel through which Sananda, Sanat Kumara and many other illumined beings and members of the White Brotherhood may reveal the will of God to the sons and daughters of Earth. In short, the highest spiritual teachings for the present day are available to all who sincerely seek the light.

"Sananda is the name for the New Age of the One who walked the Earth as the Master Jesus. He directed Sister Thedra to introduce the name, Sananda, to the world. Those familiar with the Christian Bible will recall the references to His new name.

"The work consists of both esoteric and esoteric aspects. The 'Gate House' is the esoteric headquarters for the Association. The esoteric aspect is the 'Temple of Sananda and Sanat Kurara.' Sister Thedra is 'Custodian of the Gate House' and 'Priestess in the Temple' and ordained by the Lord God Sananda. As an active channel or prophetess she is in daily communication with Sananda and other Great Ones. These communications or teachings are referred to as the Scripts, now numbering thousands of pages. As directed by Sananda, Scripts are freely given to all who ask."

In May of 1971 Charles Hillinger of the *Los Angeles Times* conducted an interview with Sister Thedra. Hillinger wrote the following:

"At Number One Vista, set in a forest of pine, is the Gate House of the Sananda and Sanat Kumura sect. A sign on the door of the large redwood headquarters cautions: 'In this house no gossiping, no flesh eaten, no dogs.'

"Sister Thedra, high priestess of this group, is a 71-year-old widow. 'I spent five years in training in the Andes of Peru before coming here,' said Thedra.

"It was Thedra who mentioned space ships from other planets regularly visiting 'the Masters on the mountain.' She displayed photo albums filled with photographs in black and white and in color of 'space ships enveloped in protective cloud cover.'"

In October, 1975, a short-lived Mount Shasta tabloid *The Shasta Union* published an interview with Sister Thedra in which she was asked to recall the circumstances that led her to the spiritual teachings she had reportedly been given. Thedra told of a near-fatal accident and a bout with lymphatic cancer. She said she addressed herself to the Lord and it was then that the One she knew as Jesus stepped through the veil, laid his hand on her, and she was instantly healed. Then she was told to go to the Andes mountains.

She also said that she was initially into sky watching and spacecraft, that her home was open for those who were interested in the New Age work, and that she was doing independent research on spacecraft and had studied almost all the books available on that subject.

During the interview she was asked how she happened to come to the Mt. Shasta area after she returned from the Andes.

She replied, "I was told to go without purse or script, just as they did in the days of old. There were five of us that came up here in a car. All had been studying with me. I was instructed to allow anyone to come who said they wanted to come." (As of this writing, Sister Thedra has moved to Arizona after having spent years in the city of Mount Shasta.)

This book would not be complete without the story of Mother Mary Maier who lived and died somewhat mysteriously.

In 1971 a headline in the weekly *Mount Shasta Herald* read: "Soul Fails to Return to Body in Trance."

In most small towns what had happened would have been an astonishing event, but in Mount Shasta it was just another in a long series of strange events.

Mother Mary Maier, 75-years-old and well-known in the community as the propri-etor of a downtown hotel known as "The Inn" had died. Nothing unusual about that, except the death of Mother Mary, who had worn flowing orange robes and sandals and was known as "Angel of the West — Guardian of the Mountain" was kept secret for a month by members of the Sree Sree Pravo sect.

During that month a 16-year-old boy and two older men stood around-the-clock guard beside her body, waiting for her soul to return.

After a full month had passed and her soul failed to return, the body was removed from the hotel to a mortuary and the inn was closed.

Who was Mother Mary Maier?

After the passage of almost two decades, no one seems to remember except that she was heavily involved with the Hindu Sree Sree Pravo group. I have in my posses-sion a proclamation from them welcoming her to India in 1966. It reads:

"To Mother Mary Mae Maier, our esteemed Mother, by the call of our almighty Father Lord 'Sree Sree Jagadbandhu Sundara,' the saviour and friend of the world, you have come again to our country after 15 long years to embrace us with your best and eternal love. You have also brought with you the message from your sweet land — the glorious land of Abraham Lincoln and the religious concern of World Fellowship.

"We are glad to receive you amidst us in our land, the land of Lord 'Sri Krishna' and the land of 'Sree Gouranga.' The Lila Bhumi of 'Sree Sree Prabhu Jagadbandhu Sundar,' the Lila Combination of All Things, the symbol of truth, love and purity.

"We show deep regard to you, Mrs. Mary Mae Maier, the true Bhakta of our Lord. You, the holy and ideal devotee of the Lord, by your charming behaviour and mother-ly affection, won the hearts of Bandhu Bhaktas of the East — so you are called by all 'Mother' and known to us as 'Mother Mary.' Our dearest Mother is anxiously waiting for Prabhu's Supreme Manifestation.

"We are sure that our Mother will be in the main role in Bandhu Sunhara's Maha Uddharan Lila. You are the Angel of the West. We sincerely say that we, the Bandhu Bhaktas of the East, will ever adorn you with garlands of our love and affection. Our doors will always remain open to you.

"We heartily believe that we are all sons and daughters of Sree Sree Prabhu Jagadbandhu Sundara and this world is our common home. We and ye are all mem-bers of the same family."

The proclamation was dated February 6, 1966, and signed with affection by mem-bers of the Sree Sree Pravoo Jagadbandhu Mahanam Pracharan Samity and Bandhu Bhakatas. It was published by the Anaadamayee Press, Calcutta, India.

Mother Mary Mae Maier, Angel of the West and Guardian of the Mountain, passed from this earthly realm in the shadow of Mt. Shasta — never to return — in 1971 at the age of 75.

Returning closer to the present, on a brilliant October morning in 1989, a woodsy area on the slopes of Mt. Shasta was transformed by a rainbow of prayer flags, color-ful Tibetan monks in maroon and gold robes, a fire of burning juniper branches, and the chanting of Buddhist prayers. And on that morning throngs of spectators awaited the arrival of the 12th Tai Situ Rinpoche, who had arranged to perform a traditional Tibetan ceremony, a purification ceremony, on Mt. Shasta.

Buddhists and non-Buddhists alike arrived in dozens of buses and hundreds of car-pools from throughout northern California and San Francisco's Bay Area to hear the words of a Tibetan lama known as the 12th Tai Situpa Rinpoche, internationally known spiritual leader who came to Mt. Shasta because, he said, "It's perfect – with all due respect to other mountains."

Before he arrived, Lama Shastri explained to those gathered the ceremony was meant to thank the earth for what it had provided, and to confess the damage humans had done in using its resources. He said the monks would also ask for the blessing of enlightened beings – that they would be praying not only for Mt. Shasta but for "all mountains and all of the oceans and all of the earth." It was also a pilgrimage for peace.

Shortly after 10 a.m., the lighting of a ritual campfire and burning of juniper boughs signaled the beginning of the centuries-old Lha Sanj ceremony after which local climbers inched up Shasta's slopes to plant traditional prayer flags on the wind-blown summit. There, the Tantric Buddhists believed the flags' ceaseless fluttering would carry prayers on behalf of all creatures to enlightened beings such as Jesus and Buddha. And they believed the winds also would carry blessings to all they touched below.

Tibetan horns announced the arrival of Tai Situ Rinpoche and crowds lined the dirt road as he walked to a stage which had been erected in the rustic setting. His head shaved and his body draped in the traditional robes of Tibetan lamas, he walked with other lamas on this pilgrimage. A small choir of Tibetan youths sang their national anthem as twelve robed lamas bowed to the master, took their places beside him on either side of a throne decorated with brilliantly colored cloth embroidered in silver and gold thread, and began a deep chant – a chant which was amplified by four speakers and reverberated off the rocky slopes above. Tibetan Buddhists believe that all things have a spirit, and the ceremony sought the cooperation of the mountain's spirit as well as that of enlightened beings.

Rinpoche and the lamas sat crosslegged on the stage and recited prayers, pausing now and then for the music of the horns, drums, and cymbals. As the hour-long cere-mony drew to a close, followers who had carried white silk scarves began tossing them hand-over-hand toward the stage in a ritual show of sincerity and purity. It was then the climbers were given the prayer flags. After they erected the flags high above, they built a fire of juniper to signal a similar rite at the site.

The 35-year-old Tai Situpa Rinpoche, also known affectionately as "precious jewel" by his followers, is highly regarded as the 12th incarnation of the Tai Situpa, the lin-eage of whom is traced to one of the chief disciples of the Guatama Buddha. (It was at the Tai Situpa Rinpoche's invitation that renowned Tibetan spiritual leader and 1989 Nobel Prize winner Dalai Lama visited San Francisco and performed the same Lha Sanj ceremony on the slopes of Mount Tamalpais.)

Asked why he brought his entourage to Mt. Shasta, Rinpoche said that he had always been impressed by the majestic beauty of Mt. Shasta on air flights above it, that "it looked perfectly balanced, just like somebody made it with lots of planning."

And he said the purpose of his pilgrimage (which included meeting with the Pope in Italy, a group of Nobel laureates in Scotland, and the Dalai Lama in San Francisco) was to spread the word about "active peace" which he said was beyond peace itself. (Note: Tibet was taken over by the Chinese in 1959 and is still under very tight control at this writing. The Tai Situpa was exiled from Tibet when he was six years old. He was permitted a visit to his homeland in 1984, met with Chinese officials, and said he was very encouraged at the time and had gained the government's permission to build 30 monasteries.)

Asked in a press interview whether his pilgrimage was in part "Eastern thought moving to the West" Rinpoche replied, "That is possible. But as the wisdom of the East moves to the West, the wisdom of the West also moves to the East. It is like two huge rivers coming together. Now we can be happy about the power and use it to benefit all people."

Finally, in his closing remarks that crisp October morning on the slopes of Mt. Shasta, Tai Situ Rinpoche of Tibet thanked the local people who had welcomed him and said, "We should also thank the spirits of this mountain. They have given us a perfect day. They recognize our intention."

Situated just outside the city limits of Mount Shasta is a 16-acre, beautifully wooded haven in which other Buddhist monks walk serenely beneath the pines and firs, long-robed and shaven headed. The 19-year-old Shasta Abbey, a Buddhist monastery in the Serene Reflection Meditation tradition, is also the headquarters of the Order of Buddhist Contemplatives which has branch communities in several cities on the west coast as well as in England and Canada.

Shasta Abbey is a Soto Zen Buddhist monastery where both men and women train for the priesthood, following the Ts'ao Tung or Soto tradition. Founded in 1970 by Reverend Roshi Jiyu-Kennett, Abbess, the Abbey also offers a variety of programs throughout the year for interested lay people of varying backgrounds and experience. These gentle Zen Buddhists live and conduct their religion unobtrusively and peacefully in their isolated pastoral retreat, and meditate often in the quiet surroundings — for the word "zen" derives from the Chinese "Ch'an" and means meditation.

Buddhism was founded in India 2500 years ago by Shakyamuni Buddha. The Zen tradition of Buddism has been transmitted from master to disciple through India, China, and Japan and is now growing in the West. Emphasizing meditation, discipline, and hard work, Zen does not rely on doctrines or scriptures but rather insists on direct religious practice and experience in daily life. In the Zen priesthood there is no discrimination with regard to race, sex, or marital status. Women can become full Zen teachers and priests may marry and have children if they wish.

In January of 1975 a bevy of friendly beagles greeted my arrival at the main gate of Shasta Abbey, and as an intercom system at the gate screens all arrivals, I waited there to be escorted into the abbey grounds. A nun hurried down to the gate, more beagle pups frolicking at her heels. We walked through the cloister and into a small entrance hall where I waited a few moments for Reverend Jitsudo Baran, the guestmaster at that time, who was going to take me on a tour of the abbey.

I remembered a quote from a book written by the abbey's founder, Reverend Jiyu Kennett: "As long as they live, trainees must live a life of purity in their monastery. The correct ordering of daily life is therefore the heart of Buddhism."

Reverend Baran led the way into the meditation room. "We meditate many times a day," he said. The meditation room was both ornate and austere. I noticed little ostentation at the abbey — monks lives are not geared toward luxury. There is, of course, immaculateness everywhere.

Reverend Baran described a routine day at the abbey: Arise at 6 a.m. (during the summer months it is not unusual to arise at 3 a.m.); meditation; morning service; clean-up; breakfast; community tea and morning lecture; work period; meditation; lunch; rest period; work period; meditation; work period; meditation; dinner; rest period; evening service; meditation. After such a full day, everyone retires early at the abbey. The routine is strictly adhered to six days a week.

We strolled in the sheltered rock-walled cloister (a beautiful, enclosed, circular, outdoor hallway which connects all buildings) and busy monks were everywhere. I had obviously arrived at a time scheduled as a work period because the sound of hammers filled the air. A short walk to the kitchen revealed that lunch was being prepared — four or five monks and nuns were concocting savory rice cakes. I was told that meals are held in complete silence; eating is considered to be part of meditation. Essentially vegetarians, they cultivate an acre of vegetables during the summer. Goats provide the abbey with milk, yogurt, and cheese. Eggs are provided by chickens and are kept for eggs only. "We do not kill," said Reverend Baran.

Zen beliefs forbid killing, adultery, falsehood, theft, the selling of liquor, the praise of self, speaking ill of others, anger, and the begrudging of charity, among other things.

I was taken to one of the shrines. Though incomplete, the room off the cloister was simple and beautiful. Because the workers were just finishing the shrine, there was no Buddha image there. It must be emphasized that, with all their admiration of Shakyamuni Buddha, his followers have never made a god of him. Shakyamuni Buddha, then, is not a god. He is the ideal of what any man may become, and the great object of Buddhism is to keep this ideal vividly in the minds of the believers.

A native of England, Roshi Jiyu-Kennet, Abbess and spiritual head of the group, explains in several books (including *How to Grow a Lotus Blossom*) the experiences of her training as a foreign woman in a Japanese temple. They include her first kensho (enlightenment experience) which is central to becoming a teacher of Zen. In the books she also explains what has previously been almost untranslatable: the seeming stages of this on-going process of meditation and training to attain enlightenment.

"A first kensho is a 'great flash of deep understanding' into the nature of God, the Cosmic Buddha, perhaps not unlike a Christian mystical experience or other intuitive revelations," she said in a 1978 interview. "It leads one into a lifetime of training and discipline to follow the precepts of God, the Cosmic Buddha."

And so, according to Zen Buddhist beliefs (which are greatly misunderstood in much of the Western world), the "Cosmic Buddha" they accept and worship is God. The Cosmic Buddha they revere is none other than God as we all know Him, with His Infinite Love, Infinite Intelligence, and Infinite Power. They believe that if they commit themselves to the Precepts — the life of inner purity and selfless giving — the love of the Cosmic Buddha will enter into their ordinary everyday lives.

When asked why they settled in the Mt. Shasta area, Reverend Baran smiled and said, "We feel nothing special about Mt. Shasta as to its being considered mystic or sacred. We do, however, certainly love the mountain for its beauty."

Since that long-ago interview, the intervening years at the abbey have been a time of putting down roots as a Western Buddhist Monastery and Sangha, with much remodeling, a new Meditation Hall, and major buildings going up one by one.

The Shasta Abbey is always open to visitors during special hours, and once a year, usually in early autumn, the public is invited to tour the monastery grounds. The tours feature the monastery's ceremony and meditation halls, the library, a formal garden and fountain area, the bell tower and huge bronze bell, the raised-bed vegetable gardens, and the cemetery (probably the only Zen Buddhist cemetery in the United States). As it is their wish to keep the land as undeveloped as possible, much of the natural rustic growth is retained; therefore the graves are located by the lay of the land rather than row by row.

Visitors find interesting the many examples of rock architecture incorporated into the buildings and walls. Refreshments are served in the garden, and usually presiding over the garden party is Reverend Roshi Jiyu-Kennet herself, the founder of the Zen Mission Society Shasta Abbey.

As Reverend Kroenke, assistant director of the monastery remarked one year, "We're a relatively large institution and some people might be wondering why we're here and what we do. This is a chance for us to welcome people in a non-religious context and let them walk around and see there are no strange or esoteric practices here that might make them uncomfortable. We don't force religion on anyone."

photo by Ed Stockton

Chapter 23

The Harmonic Convergence, Mt. Shasta - 1987

On the eve of the Harmonic Convergence, the motels were booked and hundreds of hikers were going up the mountain. A Mount Shasta Ranger District spokesman said the people were camping where he had never seen them camp. They were quiet and they were peaceful.

At the dawn of a New Age of peace and enlightenment, Harmonic Convergers meditated, danced, sang, chanted, and drummed at the world's sacred sites on the weekend of August 16th and 17th, 1987, and Mt. Shasta was considered to be one of those sacred sites. Throughout the world they also gathered at such "power points" as the Black Hills of South Dakota; the Egyptian pyramids; Machu Picchu, Peru; Chaco Canyon, New Mexico; Sedona, Arizona; Jerusalem, Israel; Chartres, France; Haleakala crater, Maui; England's Stonehenge and Avebury circles (stone shrines built by ancient cultures as centers of their civilizations and said to hold inexplicable magnetic force fields); St. Peter's Basilica in Rome, and other faraway places.

The Harmonic Convergence event came about — and just in time, it was believed — to usher in a time of increased spiritual unfoldment and a New Age of peace for mankind. "Harmonic Convergence" was a phrase coined by Jose Arguelles, a Boulder, Colorado, art historian who wrote *The Mayan Factor* and the planned convergence was anticipated as a "mass meditation" for world peace, understanding, and the purification of the earth, based on Maya and Aztec lore, Hopi Indian prophecies, and even Egyptian, Eastern, and Christian prophecies.

Arguelles had been studying the Maya Calendar for more than 30 years. As a boy growing up in both the United States and Mexico, he became interested in the Maya calendar and at age 13 he returned to Mexico and was immensely drawn to the pyramids and ancient civilization, especially to the Maya calendar and mathematical system.

Arguelles said the 468-year Aztec calendar (which ended in 1987) is derived from the Maya calendar, which has a 5100-year cycle, ending in 2012. So, according to Arguelles, in addition to being the end of one cycle, 1987 was the beginning of another 25-year cycle which would end the Maya calendar. He stated that memorable events are said to occur at cycle changes, and on August 16th, 1987, a particular vibration or frequency would be emanated by the earth and it would be perceived in many ways. Other scholars say that three ancient civilizations — the Egyptians, the Incas and the Mayas — developed separate from each other but had many similarities. They were all great builders, they made significant advances in our world, and they each created a calendar to reflect their research and to express the knowledge they had developed (separate from each other, remember) about our universe. The scholars feel these ancient cultures were very spiritual. On April 11th, 1987, the Egyptian calendar, located in the Grand Gallery of the Great Pyramid, came to an end, thus marking the end of an age.

From studying the Maya calendar and writings, Arguelles saw a 25-year phase of earth cooperation (rather than conflict), and it would begin on August 16th, 1987.

It is important to note that the ancient craftsmen who created those calendars did not just create until they ran out of stone. They were very specific and their work reflected much study, concentration and the inspection of the universe. And all cultures agreed that at the end of the calendar ages a better, purer, and more dynamic era would come into focus, an age of truth and enlightenment — if earthlings would cooperate.

Enter the Harmonic Convergence. It was a major event all over the world and, according to Arguelles, the best thing that could happen from the point of view of the earth. He believed the most intense changes would be occurring between 1987-1992. The 5100-year cycle of the Maya would reach its conclusion in 2012, and he believed this would be an opportunity to hook up with interplanetary civilizations — that is, if humans could clean up their act.

Believers said from 1987 on, people would see more things in the skies, like UFO's. Cataclysms very likely would befall the earth and unexplained coincidences would occur on a world scale. It would be a 25-year period of resonant dissonance in which the earth, according to Arguelles, could shake itself into smaller bodies unless we harmonically converged our spirits to halt the vibrations.

The Harmonic Convergence was just the start. People gathered worldwide to usher in a new consciousness of harmony, love, and unity, and to allow the human race to shift from a civilization based on materialism to a consciousness focused on the higher purposes of the planet earth.

According to literature provided in 1987 by the local (Mount Shasta) Harmonic Convergence committee, the Mayas described five phases for earth: Nature presents itself; man learns from nature; man transforms nature; nature evaluates man's transformation; man and nature synthesize. Arguelles stated that according to the Maya calendar, the fourth phase would last between 1987 and 1992, therefore August 16th and 17th of 1987 marked the entrance into that five-year stage, a five-year purification of the earth by earthquake, flood and fire. In 1992 earthlings would enter another 20-year phase, the last 20 years of the entire Mayan Great Cycle which began in 3113 BC. When the cycle closes out in 2012 AD, the shift will be to evolutionary patterns and what Arguelles calls the "galactic federation" — then, perhaps a Golden Age.

In the city of Mount Shasta on the eve of the Harmonic Convergence, all the motels were booked and there were hundreds of believers going up the mountain. Campers had been directed to the Bunny Flat and Red Fir Flat areas on the mountain. The Panther Meadows campground (day use) was always full and others camped in Squaw Creek Meadow. A Mount Shasta Ranger District spokesman said that people were camping where he had never seen them camp. They were quiet, they were peaceful. Channeling sessions (available to the public for fees up to $35) were scheduled on Mt. Shasta and other locations.

The act of channeling involves the taking over of a human's body and/or mind by an ascended master or other entity who has a message to deliver to mankind. Channelers have always been drawn to Mt. Shasta because they believe the mountain to be an extremely powerful site. People on the spiritual path are also drawn to Mt. Shasta, considered by many to be one of the most sacred places on earth.

There are three kinds of channeling: full body, conscious, and trance channeling. "Full body" occurs when the soul of the human totally leaves the body and enables the ascended master, entity, or being to incarnate and use the body fully as his (or her) own. In full body channeling there is no interference with the consciousness of the human, therefore the information being presented by the "being" is considered pure.

In the "conscious" form of channeling, the human does not go into a trance state or leave the body. In other words, the person is fully present but has the gift of concentration so deep that he or she is able to provide a vehicle for the "being" to work through, remaining fully aware while the being is talking through the body.

As for "trance" channeling, this type enables an ascended master or other being to talk through and/or utilize the body. The person normally is not conscious in the usual sense and remains in the body along with his or her energy.

Business was brisk and channelings were slated through September 1st. (Channeling was introduced nationwide when Shirley MacLaine's book *Out on a Limb* was made into a movie and aired on network television.)

In tourist-oriented Mount Shasta city, residents are accustomed to unconventional visitors arriving to commune on fabled Mt. Shasta, but not between 4,000 to 5,000 on one weekend. That's more than the population. Parking along the road up the mountain was bumper-to-bumper and there were convergers from distant places, New York, Florida, Texas, Washington, and even Canada. Most were from California, however.

All major newspapers and television networks covered the event and the Mt. Shasta gathering attracted reporters from as far as Philadelphia, Boston, Chicago, New York, San Francisco, and Los Angeles. Convergers included people from all walks of life, rich and poor alike. Most spent the night meditating.

One was quoted as saying, "The upheaval predicted in Maya, Aztec, and Hopi lore will be a physical and spiritual change — we're taking it as a positive change. After the floods and earthquakes, there will be peace and we'll live differently than we did before." Another said she had thought the earth was doomed until she learned the Mayas had predicted that mankind would change, clean the environment, and focus energy on demilitarizing world-wide — that those gathered at that sunrise Harmonic Convergence and those at other power points throughout the planet were simply planting the seeds, and that the seeds would grow. If they were not successful, she said, only nuclear disaster and other abominations await the human race.

To add to the potential impact of the convergence, the astrological perspective for August 17th, 1987, indicated a grand trine in fire signs, with Sun, Mercury, Venus and Mars in Leo; Jupiter in Aries; Saturn and Uranus in Sagittarius; plus Scorpio, Pluto sextile Neptune in Capricorn; Moon in Gemini opposing Uranus, sextile Jupiter. This planetary alignment, it was said, gave entities outside the earth a chance to help mankind focus energy for good and for peace.

Furthermore, the ancient prophecies of ancient Meso-America pinpointed the return of Quetzalcoatl, Lord of the Dawn, to the time that correlated with the Harmonic Convergence on August 16th and 17th, 1987, in the Gregorian calendar.

Quetzalcoatl, according to those who have studied this lore, represents the force of cosmic intelligence — the spiral, serpentine pattern that governs the movement of all things in this universe. Quetzalcoatl, then, is the enlightened state, the kundalini energy soaring to the crown chakra.

Meanwhile, an unexpected and extraordinary "happening" occurred within the city of Mount Shasta, whose residents have long since grown accustomed to happenings. It seemed to be a spiritual message emanating from an unlikely medium. On Friday evening before the Harmonic Convergence, the image of an angel suddenly appeared on Mount Shastan Diane Boettcher's television set. She switched channels and even unplugged the cable, and the angel remained.

As word spread, convergers and non-convergers flocked to Boettcher's video shrine. By Sunday the line had spilled out into the street and some of the neighbors became noticeably upset because of the traffic on the otherwise quiet street.

The glowing angel image appeared on her television about 11 p.m. on the Friday night before the Harmonic Convergence, as she was switching channels. Though at first it seemed to be a blast of light, the angel image remained, superimposed over the normal cable television programming, as she continued to watch.

Thinking that maybe there was a problem with her set — but also realizing the image looked like an angel — Boettcher eventually turned the television off and went to bed. But the angel image was still there in the morning. She called some friends in to see it and they agreed the image was an angel, an electronic angel.

Almost immediately the thousands who had arrived for the Harmonic Convergence, plus area residents near and far, turned the little house into a sort of shrine. Most were convinced that the angel was truly a manifestation of the divine. Boettcher summoned a channel named Solara, and Solara identified the television image as the "Angel of the Presence" who, through channeling, revealed a message which was printed and distributed to thousands on the weekend of the Harmonic Convergence. The following is the message, exactly as it was printed:

"Beloved humanity of planet Earth, I am the Angel of the Presence. I am the Angel who is found within the heart of the Essence of each of you. I am the Angel who containeth all Angels, as a bouquet of flowers containeth myriad blossoms woven together into one glorious display. I am the One; I am the Many. I am the Angel of the Presence.

"I have appeared before you now because you are finally ready to receive me. I have come as the Herald of the resplendent Golden Dawn which doth arise. I have come to announce the birth of Heaven upon Earth. Above all, I have come to issue the Call for the Angels within you to awaken. As you see me, as you feel my electrical currents pulsate throughout your cells, please allow yourself to bring me inside, for I am you. I am that which you truly are — a pulsating, shimmering rainbow being of Light, radiating limitless Love and Harmony. As you perceive these qualities in my image, please recognize them in yourself, for I am you.

"You may find it amusing that I have appeared to you on a television set, but is this not the most appropriate method for us to demonstrate the melding of Heaven and Earth? If Angels can appear in the densest matter, then we have clearly manifested the penetration by what has been termed the realm of the Spirit into the third dimensional world. This marks the birth of the Fourth Dimension on planet Earth! This breakthrough represents a quantum leap in consciousness by humanity for a major doorway has thus been opened. This has been made possible by your devoted, collective efforts in lightening and transmuting the previous levels of density. We of the Angelic realms shower you with loving gratitude for helping us to penetrate the doorway between Spirit and Matter and birth the New Age.

"The place of this penetration is within the Heart. See the expanding rays of Light emanating from my heart center. Bring me within you and feel your vast heart expand and radiate with mine. My beloved ones, know you of the vast Love that I and my Angelic Brethren have for all humanity? It is limitless and unconditional. It is Love merged with Wisdom, innocent and pure. Let our Love penetrate your beings and revitalize your cellular structures. Let our Love fling open your hearts. Let our Light free you from the bondage of the illusion of separation. For as I am the One and the many – so are you.

"I, THE ANGEL OF THE PRESENCE, shall be appearing in many third dimensional guises. Look for me on your computer screens, your television sets, and beaming down from your satellites. You shall also find me in the sky as a cloud. You shall see me in the faces of those you pass by on the street. And if we have fulfilled our mission of service to Earth, you shall recognize me in your mirror, in the sweetest Love pouring forth from your eyes.

"Yes, dear ones, let it be known that the angels are truly here on Earth."

I had passed that little house on South A street in Mount Shasta hundreds of times, never particularly noticing it. Nor did anyone else until the weekend of the Harmonic Convergence and the appearance of the angel on the television screen, when thousands poured into it. I was one of them.

As I entered the living room (the front door was wide open), a young girl was meditating on the floor in front of the television. Others came in, sat down on the floor, and assumed the yoga position (knees folded under, forefinger and thumbs touching, eyes closed). There were but two chairs in the small room, almost always occupied.

A large stained-glass creation of Jesus hung in a sunny window. White lace curtains fluttered gently. In front of the television screen was a low table full of gifts from visitors – fruit, flowers (garden flowers and some wildflowers, probably from the upper slopes of Mt. Shasta), and atop the television were vases of roses, candles, pictures of Jesus, crystals – more gifts from visitors who had come to ponder or to meditate upon this ethereal angelic vision.

All eyes in the room were staring intently at the vision in beautiful pastels – lavender, pink, the palest of greens and blues – as the angel rolled downward and off the screen, only to emerge from the top again, her wings stretching out to both sides of the television screen. Periodically, a multi-colored column appeared in the center and funneled outward. The rest of the screen was in soft shades of grey. Her face was not discernable, her arms were visible, and near the center of her waist was the purest, the most luminous whitest of whites.

A small child touched the screen reverently and the angel seemed to pulsate radiantly. A teenaged girl, overcome with emotion, moaned, cried and was stilled.

No one talked. All were silent as we watched the angel. I leaned against a back wall and perused a bookshelf. Side by side were many New Age books, plus *A Dweller on Two Planets* by Phylos the Tibetan; *The Gospel According to Thomas*; *The Portable Nietzsche*; *The Tree of Life*; *The I Ching* and other quality books.

Quietly, I left the room. Outside were many visitors, some coming, some going. (It is estimated that four to six thousand visitors, including repeats, visited the Boettcher home during the Harmonic Convergence weekend.)

"What do you think of all this?" I asked a young man who was sitting on the grass outside.

"The event is eternal to those who come here," he said reflectively. And then he added, "The eternal is secondary to the spiritual work that is being done here, however."

And then, quite suddenly, the happening ended. A local television repair man made national news by stating the angel was nothing but a broken capacitor in the set. He said he could simulate the problem on another set by disconnecting the capacitor and he did. What he produced was not nearly as beautiful as the Boettcher angel. Some agreed that it was "generically similar" — but those who continued to view the angel remained convinced that what had happened with Boettcher's television had been created by divine intervention.

By the end of the Harmonic Convergence week, Boettcher and her friends decided it was time to turn off the television and put it away. Media reporters from all over the United States (including one from the *National Observer*), plus thousands of people, had come to her home for more than a week. It was time to end it. She had even decided to move from the little white house. She admitted that it had been an incredible experience; a lot of the visitors had wonderful spiritual experiences. One of them said, "The point of the whole thing is that the angel is within us all. We can't look for it outside."

Another said, "Conventional science, in the main, continues to reject or neglect paranormal phenomena. It remains mostly for independent researchers to undertake their own investigations into this area. While conclusions may not be firmly established, a vast body of data has been accumulated by painstaking research over many years by well-qualified persons whose findings are in agreement in many respects, findings which strongly support the existence of an invisible region or "other world" which impinges upon and affects our visible lives and our own world of material concerns, more than we realize."

Indeed, angels are regarded as very real. Many have intuitively sensed their presence, their protection, and even their guidance at times. Therefore, many believe it is possible that an unknown agent, unaccounted for, can also manifest the same effect.

For awhile, a sign on Diane Boettcher's front door read: "The event is over. May the angels be with you! The house is closed. Thank you for your blessings. So be it."

Chapter 24

Elizabeth Clare Prophet Visits Mt. Shasta

Lake Siskiyou,

secluded

and jewel like.

A cool

summer retreat.

The year was 1975. Elizabeth Clare Prophet's followers had come to Mt. Shasta from all over the United States, from Trinidad, France, Africa, and other faraway places. Some spoke of entering the fiery matrix of Mt. Shasta in spirit and communion with the Brotherhood, for they believed that "Mother Prophet" was a messenger of the Ascended Masters and the Great White Brotherhood.

Elizabeth Clare Prophet — at that time thirtyish, redhaired, slim and attractive — brought her flock to the mountain because it is considered to be one of the retreats of the Ascended Masters, along with the Himalayas and the Grand Tetons. Intelligent and well-educated, she held a Bachelor of Arts in political science. She stated that she and her late husband, Mark, had been in contact with an Ascended Master named El Morya since they were children.

And it was El Morya who directed Mark and Elizabeth to found the Summit Lighthouse organization in 1958. Their followers became known as "Keepers of the Flame," meaning they strive to keep the flame of Christ's spirit in their hearts.

It became obvious to local residents that the Keepers of the flame movement closely resembled the I Am Activity or Saint Germain Foundation, the religious group that originally centered on Mt. Shasta. Guy Ballard, founder of the I Am Activity claimed to have been instructed by Saint Germain after they had met beside a forest stream on the slopes of Mt. Shasta in 1930.

St. Germain, it was pointed out in interviews that weekend, was indeed a key figure in the list of Ascended Masters in Elizabeth Clare Prophet's organization, and it was agreed the two organizations shared the belief in Ascended Masters, non-violence, patriotism and the belief that people are capable of great good (and power) if they are taught by messengers of the Ascended Masters. (Note: After Ballard's death, his wife, Edna, became chief messenger for the I Am Activity. After her death in the early 1970s, Frederick Landwehr assumed the responsibility.)

Among the brochures and pamphlets heralding Elizabeth Clare Prophet's arrival in the Mt. Shasta area was *Shasta 1975 — A Conference for Spiritual Freedom* in which Ascended Master St. Germain welcomed the group in these words:

Cave of Symbols
Gemini 1975

To All Who Love Freedom, Hail!

A conference for spiritual freedom is truly the need of the hour. For while the defenses of material freedom are wasting away on the boundaries of a planet, in the souls of a people a true spiritual freedom must be wrought.

I come as the Hierarch of the Aquarian Age and I come as the humble servant of the light of freedom within you. To all who would preserve that freedom, both spiritually and materially, I say, Welcome to Shasta 1975! I am your host for four days of communion in the Lord's Spirit, and I am also the host of many masterful beings who have ascended into the light of freedom who are gathering for this communion of devotees.

The program includes dictations from the heavenly hosts to be given through the messenger of the Great White Brotherhood, Elizabeth Clare Prophet, whom I sponsored long ago to be the mouthpiece of hierarchy in this period of transition between Pisces to Aquarius. Lectures by the messenger will set forth the principles of cosmic law which must be practiced and protected if this nation and any nation are to endure in the flame of freedom. Masters and cosmic beings will speak to humanity to define universal truth and its immediate application to world dilemma.

To all who cherish liberty and the dream of freedom at home and in the world community, to all who would defend cosmic consciousness as the right of every man, woman, and child, again I say, Welcome to Shasta 1975! I shall see you there. May you be blessed with the vision of the Lord's hosts.

In the flame I remain,

Saint Germain

Two thousand strong they came to the sacred mountain over the Fourth of July weekend in 1975. The enormous tent which housed their meditations, lectures and dictations from the heavenly hosts (through the messenger of the Great White Brotherhood, Elizabeth Clare Prophet) went up in the sunny expanse of the Lake Siskiyou campgrounds amidst tall pines, a stone's throw away from the exquisite alpine lake which reflected Mt. Shasta in its waters.

They journeyed from all over the world to participate in a program which included, over the long weekend, dictations from Ascended Master Saint Germain, Jesus the Christ, Godfre Ray King, Kuthumi Lai Singh, Cyclopea, Pallus Athena, Surya and Cuzco, The Master of the Mountain, The Old Man of the Hills, and others. Masters and cosmic beings spoke through Mother Prophet.

The Great White Brotherhood, it should be pointed out, is purported to be those immortals who have mastered the laws of their own karma and have taken their place among the hosts of the Lord. They have mastered time and space and are said to have been thrust from the rebirth cycle. They are said to have transcended planes of consciousness, have "ascended" into the light of freedom, and are now dedicated to the salvation of all mankind through the major religions of the world.

"The Brotherhood of Mt. Shasta," according to one of Mother Prophet's informative brochures, "is part of the Great White Brotherhood. Its members hail from an ancient hierarchy of light-bearers who were there when Mu went down. They are ascended and unascended masters who keep the flame of purity in the mountain and receive chelas who meet the measure of their rod. They are devotees of Buddha and his light. They are disciplined priests and priestesses who tended the flame of the Mother on the altars of Mu before she sank. They are Zoroastrians and Confucians,

Taoists and Zen monks. They chant of the AUM and are well acquainted with mystery of the Christos in the I AM THAT I AM."

In an interview with Jerome Armstrong, Jr., who handled public relations for the group at that time, he explained, "The Great White Brotherhood certainly does not indicate racism. We do not discriminate. God does not discriminate against himself. Actually, the White Brotherhood means the 'white light of the Christ' — the perfect balance of all the rays."

The next day at Lake Siskiyou I talked to one of Mother Prophet's followers. Though I was familiar with many of the metaphysical and other spiritual groups who considered the mountain to be sacred, the Keepers of the Flame were unknown to me. I was told that this unique nondenominational religious and philosophical organization was founded in Washington, D.C., in 1958 by the Master El Morya of Darjeeling, India, through messengers Mark and Elizabeth Clare Prophet; that the organization planned to establish teaching centers world-wide, and was to be known as "Summit Lighthouse International" with headquarters in Colorado Springs. The west coast center was located in Santa Barbara, California.

"Why was the conference held in the Mt. Shasta area?" I asked. He seemed reluctant to answer that, saying he was not the spokesman for the group. And then, as he looked up to the mountain, he said slowly, "Mt. Shasta is an ancient focus of light for the entire planetary body. It is a spiritual center. It has a certain aura which surrounds it and we can feel the radiation from it. It draws many people to it who are not even aware of its significance."

From the area of the campground came the strains of "Ave Maria" and upon entering, I found several thousand quiet, well-disciplined members. Many were already inside the cavernous tent. Many were sitting outside in a semi-lotus position with palms up (not an unfamiliar sight to Mount Shastans) and everywhere peace and decorum prevailed. Young and old, black and white, Japanese and Chinese mingled in perfect harmony.

I had unwittingly timed my visit to coincide with a "dictation" and a meditative hush had fallen on the crowd. Not knowing exactly what to do, I stood silently in the warm July sun and waited. Suddenly the clear voice of Elizabeth Clare Prophet came over the public address system. I tried to move closer to the tent opening so that I could see the Mother of the Flame, as she was called. I was stopped immediately and told in a kindly manner that I must retreat, the dictation had started. This dictation, scheduled at four o'clock on Friday afternoon, was from Pallas Athena, Goddess of Truth.

I checked my program. It was the scheduled four o'clock meditation and dictation. Under "Pallas Athena: Goddess of Truth" was written: "The oracles of Delphi were messengers of the gods and goddesses who spoke truth and the wisdom of the law to the ancients. Pallas Athena is more than a Grecian goddess of mythology. Her presence in the universe is the exaltation of the flame of living truth. This truth she holds on behalf of the evolutions of earth as a member of the Karmic Board. The Karmic Board is the Supreme Court for this system of worlds, its seven members adjudicate world and individual karma. They review the actions of mankind lifetime after lifetime. It is they who determine who shall embody when and where. They assign souls to families and communities, and they measure out the weights of karma that must be balanced as the jot and tittle of the law."

After the dictation, the strains of a mighty organ flowed through the pines. Everyone was standing now, palms up. Some wore long robes, some wore long dresses or pantsuits, and many of them wore white because it was Friday. (Sunday, yellow; Monday, pink; Tuesday, blue; Wednesday, green; Thursday, purple and gold; Friday, white; Saturday, violet.) Students were not to wear black, red, red-orange, chartreuse, or fuchsia, and they should avoid wearing brown, grey, or olive. Colors, to members, were associated with rays and vibrations; furthermore, everyone should present themselves in clothing which would be respectable before the hierarchy, and also before one another.

People streamed from the over-sized tent. They would have their evening meal and then gather again at eight o'clock that same evening for a dictation from St. Germain. In another tent labeled the "Garden of Eden," food and soft drinks were dispensed — all vegetarian, of course. Some students went to their tents and campers, while others drove to their motel rooms in the village of Mount Shasta, less than three miles away.

I wandered over to the information booth and again sought out Jerome Armstrong, Jr. "This organization is, then, a spin-off of the local I Am Activity?" I asked.

He frowned ever so slightly. "The Master St. Germain," he replied, "who founded the I AM Activity is also the founder of our organization, though ours is different. Many of our teachings are similar to theirs, many are not."

Further conversation revealed that the Keepers of the Flame were intensely patriotic (five American flags whipped in the breeze atop the meeting tent), were extremely non-violent, they were taught that they are capable of great goodness and that everyone can attain illumination. Armstrong invited me to come back the following day at four o'clock for "The Brotherhood of Mt. Shasta" session in which the Master of the Brotherhood of Shasta would speak through Mother Elizabeth and for the first time reveal his name to a public audience. This was to be a special gift to the students. Also, The Old Man of the Hills would speak through Elizabeth Clare Prophet. I was given a large packet of literature to peruse and a special press pass which would prevent my being stopped so many times both inside and outside the Lake Siskiyou campgrounds. (Curious outsiders were courteously but firmly discouraged. Students registered months in advance and paid $36 each for the privilege of attending the conference.)

Arriving promptly at four o'clock the next day, tape recorder in hand, I went directly to the large tent. I was stopped before entering and told I was not to tape the dictation. Not to tape? Why did they think I was there? Appealing to Armstrong, he agreed that I was not to tape the dictation, but he promised to mail me a copy along with permission to print it (which he did).

Already on the blue-carpeted, blue-draped stage was Elizabeth Clare Prophet and this was my first glimpse of her.

Also on the stage was a large, lighted world globe, an organ, and a piano. Flanking the lectern were two massive ornate chairs. An American flag was raised to the left. Centered in back of the lectern, in full color, was a monumental reproduction of Mt. Shasta. Two large candelabras sent flickering shadows on the larger-than-life portraits of Jesus Christ and St. Germain. The summer breeze playfully caused the huge tent to lift and swell as though it were alive.

Clad in a long white gown enhanced by a glittering necklace which I assumed was a diamond necklace, Elizabeth Clare Prophet was seated in one of the chairs. Eyes closed, hands gripping the arms of the chair, she seemed to be in deep meditation.

Soft music flowed from the public address system while students filed quietly into the tent.

When all were seated, Mother Prophet arose and walked to the lectern. Again she closed her eyes. Finally her head raised heavenward. Absolute silence prevailed inside the tent; it was as though everyone had become hypnotized.

I was impressed. This diminutive, auburn-haired figure, almost dwarfed in front of the huge, inspiring picture of majestic Mt. Shasta, seemed to be in perfect harmony with her followers. She was electrifying.

Then the dictation from the "Master of the Mountain" began, her voice a semi-monotone, lowering at times to almost a whisper. The following was the dictation in which the Master of the Mountain revealed his name:

"I AM the voice of the mountain. I come to bear tidings of the Brotherhood of Mt. Shasta unto all who have been called and all who have answered the call at inner levels and in outer manifestation. I come forth from the heart of the mountain and from the heart of your own I AM Presence to welcome you into the fiery core of purity, to welcome you into the fraternity of souls of light-bearers.

"Hail, children of Mu! Hail, children of the Motherland! You have come home to our abode, and here we have kept the flame for many thousands of years. Here we have coalesced fiery energies of consecration from the altars of Mu and placed them upon the altar of the mountain.

"I AM Ra Mu. That is my name. I release it unto you that you might give the chant that is sung by devotees of our holy order, that you might intone the name that God has given unto my own I AM name, a name that is a chalice for the ray of the Motherland to be drawn forth now from the heart of a mountain into the hearts of devotees assembled in the physical octave. And, therefore, those at etheric levels who are members of our order who have intoned that holy sound, rejoice and look forward to the intoning of that sound with you that day — that day that has come now as the day of rejoicing here at the foot of our holy mountain.

"As you have listened unto the music and the singing and the voices, know that choirs of beings, devotees of ancient Lemuria, Ascended Masters and their chelas who have gathered in the retreat of Mt. Shasta were anchoring through that sound, by the action of the light and sound ray, into this octave chorus of the ancient music of the Motherland, that you might be quickened in the intonation of the AUM, into the divine memory of your origin and your life on Mu, and how you served the Ancient of Days, and how you served the holy Kumaras and Lady Master Venus.

"Now then, as I have given to you my name, will you not use it as a chant of love whereby the light of Mu and of Shasta and of the momentum of devotees of the ages can be anchored in a moment in your heart for service? And my own causal body I place upon the altar of the Great White Brotherhood, that it might be used as a magnet to draw the souls who serve together in the mandala of the Motherland once again to that point of intimate communion in the Holy Spirit, so that that light can stream forth in all of its intensity, in all of its love, to capture souls — young souls on Terra, older souls and embodied angels, elemental life — to capture them all in the central flame of the Mother which we enshrine."

At this point in the dictation, the audience joined the Master of the Mountain in chanting "Ra Mu" three times. Then Ra Mu continued the dictation, using Elizabeth Clare Prophet as his channel:

"The sounding of the word rolls up the mountain, and the sounding of the word by the devotees of the mountain resounds and flows down the mountainside. And the meeting of the waves of light is the rejoicing of light and of the waves of Alpha and Omega as devotees ascended and unascended, devotees of inner planes and outer consciousness, merge in the devotion of the one fire of Shasta. Wherever you are, wherever you make your abode and your altar, know that when you sound the name that I bear, the light will flow from Shasta, from my causal body to your own fiery heart. And thus the oneness of cycles and the ritual of that oneness is commenced this day.

"I pay tribute to all who have served the light and I acknowledge many friends of light and of the mountain who have been a part of the inner experience of the mystery school that is conducted here in our retreat. Coming in the physical to this conference, making the pilgrimage to the physical focus, will also serve to anchor in your outer mind those experiences which you have had here, the instruction, and also that which has been given in the Grand Teton Retreat.

"Now I would speak to you of other evolutions and of other lifewaves coming nigh Terra and the signal of those lifewaves as the signs written in the heavens, written in the stars, and written in the clouds. I would speak to you of great civilizations of light-bearers, of nuclei of souls who inhabit various planes of consciousness in Terra, of the beings who inhabit the earth itself — a masterful race, those who also descended from Lemuria. And the interconnection of these lifewaves to our retreat is secure.

"Mankind does not realize how Terra is honeycombed with retreats and life-waves and evolutions. You are on the surface. Many are within. Many enjoy the light of the sun of the fiery core even as you enjoy the light of Helios and Vesta. The Brotherhood of Mt. Shasta seeks the integration by the action of the eighth ray of all hearts who are afire with the love of bringing earth into that point of initiation of the resurrection and the ascension.

"These are souls serving diligently in many planes of consciousness having the celestial body, the etheric body, as you have the terrestrial or earthly body. Simply by dialing a frequency of consciousness, as many evolutions in this and other solar systems are able to do, you could advance to their plane of awareness. You could pass through the mountain by the adjustment of the dial of frequency and even enter, retaining physical consciousness, our retreat. And yet this knowledge has not been vouchsafed to the majority of those living on the surface of Terra; for they have not shown the mastery of the God-control, the God-harmony of the fiery core. For once that fiery core is released for the adjustment of atomic frequencies, tremendous power comes into integration in the four lower bodies. And the awareness of God-reality in the face of all that assails that power must be the mastery of the chela on the path.

"On the path then to our retreat, if you would come retaining physical awareness there are yet hurdles to be passed. Others have passed them; others are studying. You may be counted among them. You may become initiates of our retreat, but there are requirements. And the first of these is Love. Love must sound the new tone of the Aquarian Age. Love is a word that is used. Let it now be a vibration that is pure. Let it be purified in the heart chakra! I send forth the light of my heart! I challenge all misuses of the fire of love! I say, let those energies now cycle in for qualification by the sacred fire!

"We will not allow the desecration of our holy mountain. We will not allow the impurity of that vibration of the misuse of love which manifests as rebellion against the wisdom teaching of the ages, against the Lord God and the Logos, against the sacred fire. We will not allow those enemies of the Real Self to camp upon the holy mountain of God.

"Therefore, from the summit of Shasta there exists now a sacred energy rolling down the mountain as golden liquid fire. So it purifies! So it inundates! So it carries the flame of devotees! And if you look in Akasha, you will behold in former times the record of volcanic eruption when that was a physical manifestation; and you will see the counterpart as the action of the overflow of the golden honey, the elixir from Venus that comes forth from the mountain of the Mother, tribute unto Mater. You will see how the etheric level of that overflow is a penetration of fire, a cleansing and an anchoring.

"So, let it be this day from etheric levels that energy goes forth! It is the energy of victory — mightier than an avalanche of snow and ice. So the golden oil rolls with a power that will not be stayed. It is a sacred fire purifying the holy mountain, challenging those who misuse the energies of our abode.

"Henceforth, then, all who walk upon the mountain shall give accounting and shall be called by the Lords of Karma for their abuse of that sacred energy. And that judgment will not be turned back, and there shall be a quickening of that victorious light contacting the heart. And those who resist it, those who blaspheme it, those who turn against the messengers of the Brotherhood — these will have their time, their place to give accounting before the hierarchy of Shasta.

"We seal Shasta in Mother light. We seal this day physical atoms, atoms at every plane. So, let it be the focal point, then, for the raising of the culture of Lemuria even as that focal point is the place of the heart of the devotee.

"Oh Shasta, crown chakra of Lemuria, of Lemurians focusing the light of God-consciousness, now release thy flame of golden light! Now release that energy! Now let mankind know that the one true God is able to raise up a mighty people, a mighty continent, a mighty following unto the glory of the I AM THAT I AM. And this precipitation of the golden elixir shall be a monument to the Great Divine Director. And it shall be for the seventh root race, for the incoming souls, a focal point of mastery and of light and of homecoming and of the welcome of the Mother flame.

"Crystal clarity of the mountain, now let the fire ascend! Now let the smoke be the vapor of the Holy Spirit! Now let it be the rising of the incense from the altars of the devotees of fire! Now let that incense be pleasing unto the Lord, a celebration of the communion of hearts 'as above, so below.' Now let it be that all evolutions and lifewaves have the contact from the physical unto the etheric, unto the Ascended Master octaves of a new momentum, a new vibration which your coming has made possible in the physical octave.

"Hail, children of Lemuria! Hail, children of the Mother! Hasten to greet the sunlight of the dawn! Hasten to seize the energy of the sun! Then run with the sun! Then run with the wind! Then run to greet your cosmic destiny at the summit of Shasta!

"I am standing at the summit — my heart, my head, and my hand forming the trinity of light. I stand to receive you. Come! Come into the heart of the holy of holies. And the way is through your I AM Presence. The way is through the open door of the Real Self.

"So, find reality and find me standing in the snowy fires of the Mother light. I AM Ra Mu."

After the dictation, Elizabeth Clare Prophet folded her hands, left the lectern, and seated herself. Her followers stood, palms up, in apparent adoration. Then she walked slowly back to the lectern where she turned and held her arms out to the mountain. Then she held her arms out to her followers, and blessed them, after which she walked slowly to the left of the stage where four youthful escorts accompanied her as she left the tent.

Many of her followers stayed in their seats, busy with note-taking or in meditative repose. The candles were extinguished onstage, and most of the crowd departed in orderly fashion to the strains of soft music.

As I left, the smoke of campfires began to permeate the area. Members gathered at their campsites for dinner, preparatory to the evening's program and a ten o'clock dictation from Alpha, who, according to the program, is the personification of the God flame as Father in the core of consciousness we call life — Alpha, the highest manifestation of God in the Great Central Sun.

There would be more dictations on Sunday (all channeled by Mother Prophet) and on the last day, Monday, a hike up Mt. Shasta to Panther Meadows for a marriage ritual for Keepers of the Flame, performed en masse by Mother Prophet. There would also be, that day, the ceremony of baptism on the mountain.

And then the four-day "Conference for Spiritual Freedom" on the shores of Lake Siskiyou ended, and the Keepers of the Flame quietly left the slopes of the mountain along with their leader, Elizabeth Clare Prophet.

Though the group has not returned to Mt. Shasta, much has changed since that peaceful summer of 1975. As of this writing, Elizabeth Clare Prophet and about 1000 of her followers, believing a possible nuclear confrontation will occur sometime after October 2nd, 1989 (and believing also that the decade of the 1990s is prophesied to be a time of great upheaval with the occurrence of a variety of cataclysmic events leading up to the year 2000, and the dawning of the Age of Aquarius) have moved to Paradise Valley, Montana. The name "Summit Lighthouse International" has been changed to the "Church Universal and Triumphant" and Mother Prophet and her followers have been in the news nationally. They have been building fall-out shelters and also have been setting up a sophisticated food-processing plant to stockpile dried vegetables and macrobiotic meat substitutes for what they think are dark days ahead.

The group (at this writing) is also being investigated for stockpiling weapons. In newspaper and television interviews, Elizabeth Clare Prophet based her predictions of doom partly on a "heavy descent of karma as prophesied in the New Testament book of Revelations," the prophecies of which, in her opinion, will bring war, plagues, famine, and economic collapse.

"We believe in surviving," said a member, speaking over the roar of work crews busily building a large underground bomb shelter on the slopes of Montana's Gallatin Mountains.

Other believers in extremely dark days ahead during the years preceding the Age of Aquarius were those involved in the 1987 international Harmonic Convergence — as well as famed prophet Nostradamus.

Chapter 25

About Other Significant Books...

Lenticular clouds

they float like

snowy silver dollars

over Mt. Shasta's

glistening peak.

Many think the mystery legends of Mt. Shasta began with a book written in 1884 entitled *A Dweller on Two Planets*. The writer, an eighteen-year-old boy, lived in Yreka, California, within sight of the mountain. His name was Frederick Spencer Oliver. But Oliver claimed that he had transcribed the entire book through automatic writing and that the book's actual author was Phylos the Tibetan. The book cover acknowledges Phylos as the author.

This occult volume is divided into three books and "Book I" deals mainly with the past incarnations of Phylos in Atlantis where, in one of them, he was known as Zailm in 11,160 B.C.

In "Book II" Phylos experienced a more recent incarnation as an American during the gold rush, under the name of Walter Pierson. During this time he met and became friends with Quong, a Chinese laborer, whose aloof demeanor set him apart from the other gold miners in the Mt. Shasta area.

Quong is actually a learned "adept" of a secret order of mystics, the Lothinian Brotherhood, who dwell within Mt. Shasta. As their friendship deepened, Quong led Pierson to a lonely canyon and a hidden entrance into the mountain. Along the way a doe and her fawn stepped into the path before them. Quong stroked them gently and as he did so a hungry mountain lion appeared ferociously before them. The doe and her fawn, in fright, pressed against Quong for protection. Quong said in a low, kindly voice to the beast, "Peace." Whereupon the lion began purring like a kitten and then tread quietly beside them on the path.

Approaching the entrance, Quong touched an enormous quadrangular block of stone. Immediately it tipped on edge and leaned outward over them, Quong controlling it through what he called mental magnetism. They entered a tunnel which led to a large circular chamber with a domelike ceiling about 60 feet wide. The walls were illuminated and polished like glass. On the floor was a carpet "of Oriental variety," the fabric of which was long fibers loosely woven. Around the sides of the chamber extended a wide divan. Quong told him the chamber was called a Sach and that there were others throughout the western hemisphere.

Pierson (Phylos) then discovers that he has been chosen to enter the order, should he choose to do so. He accepts, and begins his long struggle toward understanding the spiritual mysteries behind eternal life. Could he attain the Lothinian purity of heart and body? The Christ-spirit? "Book II" recounts his experiences, and also his astral visit to Venus.

In "Book III" Phylos ponders the scenes of his Atlantean lives, the lives of the two ladies he loved, and also how karma had exacted pay. He realized finally that the lesson in life is "whatsoever a man soweth, that shall he also reap." This final book also tells of the fall of mighty Atlantis, once known in prehistoric times as Atlan, "Queen of the Seas," and her people as "Children of Incal" (Incal meaning God), numbering at home and abroad in the colonies almost 300 million souls. Days and nights of horror came; mountains fell upon the plains, tidal waves and floods swept throughout the land. Then the final tremble and the great continent of Atlantis sank to the bottom of the ocean,

Why? Phylos tells of corruption and the lust for riches and power that had already fatally weakened "the proudest people the earth has ever known." And then earthquakes shook the continent until all things sank — down, down, down, into the restless sea.

A Dweller on Two Planets is by far the most important book — actually a minor classic — relating to the development of the Mt. Shasta legend-cycle, and those who have made serious studies of the ensuing flood of books containing accounts of mystical happenings on Mt. Shasta say that some of the authors of said books seem to have drawn rather heavily on this original book, which was written in 1884.

The Lost Continent of Mu by Colonel James Churchward (mentioned earlier in the chapter describing the Castle Creek petroglyphs) was written in 1931 and has had dozens of printings since. Churchward's apparent objective in writing this very informative book was to prove beyond any doubt that the continent of Mu (Lemuria) existed and that a highly advanced civilization dwelled there until it sank into the depths of what is now known as the Pacific Ocean.

In this book are hundreds of illustrations showing relics from Mu; symbols and vignettes found on ancient Naacal tablets; the first book ever written; a Troano manuscript recounting the destruction of Mu; Mu's hieratic alphabet; the geographical position of Mu; maps of Mu and graphics realistically portraying the submersion of Mu. Plus relics of Maya, Aztec, Egyptian, Easter Island and other ancient civilizations, because, as Churchward explained, they all evolved from the Motherland of Mu, the cradle of civilization, "The Empire of the Sun."

Churchward based his convictions on the translations of two sets of ancient tablets — Naacal tablets which he discovered in India, plus a large collection (2500) of stone tablets discovered many years ago in Mexico by William Niven. Both sets, he writes, have the same origin; both sets are extracts from the *Sacred Inspired Writings of Mu*.

Churchward tells of Mu, a strange country of 64 million inhabitants who had developed a superior civilization and was at the height of her magnificence 50,000 or more years ago. Mu was an immense continent which covered half of what is now the Pacific Ocean, and was thousands of miles long. The very southern tip contained what is now Easter Island (with its 555 carved statues), some of which did not sink. Churchward tells of the dominant people of Mu, a white race. But besides this race, there were other races, people with black, yellow, or brown skin. The ancient inhabitants of Mu were excellent navigators and sailors who took their ships all over the world. They were also learned architects, building great temples and palaces of stone, carving and setting up great monoliths as monuments. The population was divided into three classes: leisure, middle, and the laboring class. The leisure, or wealthy classes, adorned themselves in jewels and fine raiment and lived in imposing palaces with many servants.

Colonies had been started in all parts of the earth, governed by Mu, the Motherland. According to Churchward, all followed the same religion, a worship of the Deity (God) through symbols. All believed in the immortality of the soul, and so great was their reverence for the Deity, they never spoke His name. In prayer and supplication He was always addressed through a symbol. For instance, "Ra the Sun" was used as the collective symbol for all His attributes, and as high priest, Ra Mu was the representative of the Deity in religious teachings, not to be worshiped, it was understood, only a representative.

While Mu was at her zenith, she received a fearful shock: rumblings from the bowels of the earth, followed by earthquakes, and many volcanoes belched forth fire and lava. But then all was serene again. Cities were rebuilt, trade and commerce resumed. But it was not to last. Generations later the entire continent heaved and rolled, the land trembled, temples and palaces and monuments crashed to the ground.

Churchward stated that "fires of the underneath" burst forth in flames three miles in diameter. All was destruction. From the Troano Manuscript and the Codex Cortesianus (a Maya book dating back to the time of the Troano Manuscript) came the following: "During the night Mu was torn asunder and rent to pieces. With thunderous roarings the doomed land sank. Down, down, down, she went, into the mouth of hell — a tank of fire.

"In one of the final chapters of this book, Churchward tells of the scientific cause of the sinking of Mu. His investigations, he wrote, proved that the calamity was due to the emptying of a series of isolated upper gas chambers (existing very near the surface) which were upholding the land, and which were probably connected to each other by cracks and fissures. He goes to great lengths to prove this theory, basing his opinion on the depths of the Pacific Ocean and his research on the *Troano Manuscript*, the *Codex Cortesianus* and the *Lhasa Record*.

Mu the Motherland sank into a watery abyss, enveloped in flames as she went down. The date of this earthly disaster was determined to be somewhat less than 15,000 years ago, or about 12,500 B.C. As she went down, other continents and islands changed suddenly and drastically. Some went down, portions of others were raised.

The Lost Continent of Mu is a worthy book, a scholarly book full of fascinating revelations of a prehistoric race beyond recall, researched over a period of 50 years by Colonel James Churchward.

There are other strange books about the mysteries of Mt. Shasta, some written in the form of novels and novelettes, and throughout the years there have been other publications written about the lost continent of Mu, or Lemuria.

A small volume entitled *The Story of Atlantis and The Lost Lemuria* by W. Scott-Elliot is actually two books in one — *The Story of Atlantis* was published in 1896 and *The Lost Lemuria* was published in 1904. The preface to the first, written by A. P. Sinnett in 1896, reveals that occult methods of investigation were used. He speaks of astral clairvoyance which had been employed to carry out the investigations upon which the book on Atlantis had been compiled.

According to the author, the destruction of Atlantis came about through a series of catastrophes varying from great cataclysms in which whole territories and populations perished, to comparatively unimportant landslips such as occur on the earth's coasts today. But after the first great catastrophe in which the main continent of Atlantis was destroyed (which took place, he said, in the Miocene age, about 800,000 years ago) there was no intermission of the landslips which slowly but steadily ate away the continent.

The second catastrophe, the author relates, occurred about 200,000 years ago. and the third — about 80,000 years ago — was extremely devastating. It destroyed all that remained of the Atlantean continent, with the exception of the island to which Plato gave the name of Poseidonis, and Poseidonis was ultimately submerged in the fourth and final great catastrophe of 9,564 B.C.

Maps are included in this book showing the earth before and after the submersions of Atlantis, and the author deals with religious beliefs, rituals, architecture, the flora and fauna, and as evidence of its existence, he quotes ancient writers Aelian, Proclus, Marcellus, Diodorus Siculus, and Plato.

As to Lemuria, the author shows two maps, one representing Lemuria and adjoining lands during the period of that continent's greatest expansion; the second map shows Lemuria's outlines after its dismemberment by great catastrophes, but long before its final destruction. Scott-Elliot points out that the Atlantean maps were produced by "adepts" in the days of Atlantis, but the origin of the Lemurian maps was hazy. They could have been fashioned by divine Lemurian instructors, or they could have been produced in the still later days of the Atlantean epoch.

In *The Lost Lemuria* the author describes the races of mankind: The First Root Race, which, being astral could leave no fossil remains; the Second Root Race which was Etheric; the Third Root Race, or Lemurian; the Fourth Root Race, or Atlantean; and the Fifth Root Race, or Aryan.

The evolution of the Lemurians is told in detail, and again we are told that Lemuria was the cradle of the human race and that man did not descend from apes. The Lemurians eventually built great cities in which they erected gargantuan buildings, temples, and palaces, which, of course, corresponded with their gigantic bodies.

Unlike the later fate of Atlantis — which was submerged by great tidal waves — Scott-Elliot relates that the continent of Lemuria perished by volcanic action. The entire land became a hell of burning ashes and the red-hot dust from numberless volcanoes. Earthquakes completed the destruction until Lemuria sank into its watery grave, a civilization lost forever.

Chapter 26

Mt. Shasta, Geologically Speaking...

A view

from

The Summit—

Solitary

Beauty

in

Mid-Winter

Cover.

"Stay up there in the rain-shadow of the sublime mountain," an admirer of Mt. Shasta recently wrote to me. "Do you know that Shasta has the largest base and the greatest mass of any lone peak in the world? Its alpenglow leaves me breathless, uplifted, and bemused always."

Indeed, my friend, Mt. Shasta's alpenglow leaves everyone breathless, and its conformation is dramatically beautiful, too, rising so directly and abruptly from the surrounding countryside. One of the largest stratovolcanoes in the world, Shasta rises to an altitude of 14,162 feet and its volume is said to be just over 80 cubic miles.

Visitors traveling to spend adventuresome days on Mt. Shasta's slopes discover that this majestic mountain can be seen in every direction for a hundred miles or more. It rises splendidly in lonely grandeur, and there are those who believe it is the most beautiful mountain in the world.

Geographically the mountain stands alone, a circumstance that heightens its scenic effect, its appearance of majestic isolation. In structure, Mt. Shasta differs materially from the adjacent ranges.

It is a true volcano. It was once thought that it was formed by volcanic activity beginning probably in early Tertiary (Eocene) time, and continued alternative active and quiet periods for millions of years. But my friend Dr. William Bridge Cooke, world renowned mycologist who spent entire summers on the mountain (a mountain man who certainly needs no introduction to the Mt. Shasta area) wrote in a letter: "As a result of the EIS necessary for the wilderness proposal, there has been a change in thinking about the dates of the formation of Mt. Shasta. Present dates state it at 700,000 years, so it is the youngest Cascade mountain and the youngest mountain in the United States — the lower 48, at least."

In 1975 the full complexity of Shasta's structure began to emerge when Drs. C. Dan Miller and Robert L. Christiansen (United States Geological Survey) spent months combing the volcano's surface. They camped five days at the summit and another five days high on Shastina and they found that Mt. Shasta consists of at least four distinct but overlapping cones which were built during four different eruptive cycles.

They later generously shared the results of their extensive Mt. Shasta field work with Stephen L. Harris, who included the findings in his book *Fire and Ice, The Cascade Volcanoes* in 1976; then in 1988 his revised edition *Fire Mountains of the West: The Cascade and Monolake Volcanoes* was published by the Mountain Press Publishing Company of Missoula, Montana. Fascinating and readable, this book tells everything you ever wanted to know about volcanoes and it's extremely interesting if you happen to live on the slopes of one of the 'fire mountains" he describes. Or even if you don't.

Mt. Shasta is not a single peak but a multiple structure. From its western flank rises 12,330-foot Shastina, which, if it stood alone would rank as the third highest mountain in the entire Cascade chain because only Rainier and Shasta, itself, rises higher.

According to Harris, Mt. Shasta is a mere infant compared to the Klamath mountains which lie over a green valley to the west of it. Rugged and beautiful in their own right, these peaks were formed of more ancient rocks and were "upheaved" into place millions of years before Mt. Shasta came into being.

He goes on to say, "The discovery that Shasta is really four volcanoes of varying age piled atop and against each other helps explain some puzzling features. Although its shape is generally symmetrical, Shasta has some irregularities and protrusions which cannot be explained by derivation from a single central vent. It has also seemed strange that the most deeply eroded and extensively glaciated parts of the mountain form its southern slopes. Because there are fewer hours of direct sunlight and less melting on the northern and eastern sides of the peaks, the largest glaciers and resulting cirques in most cases occur on the shaded north and east sides, as they do on McLoughlin, Hood, Adams, and Rainier."

During the 10,000-12,000 years since the Pleistocene glaciers melted in this part of California, Mt. Shasta added both the parasitic cone of Shastina and the present summit cone to its mass, and Harris goes into detail about the building of Shastina on its

Drs. C. Dan Miller and Robert L. Christiansen camped five days on the mountain's summit and another five days on Shastina, combing the volcano's surface. This aerial view shows the arctic or nival zone of Mt. Shasta. On all other California peaks, the alpine belt extends to the summit. That centered dark spot is the sulphurous hot spring that boils near the summit. Photo by Neil & Carl Clement.

west flank. (Shastina is Shasta's seldom-visited satellite peak with a nearly mile-wide summit crater containing a beautiful turquoise lake.) Harris also states that Black Butte, the spectacular hornblende dacite plug dome at Shasta's western base probably dates from this eruptive episode.

Black Butte, which looms alongside Interstate 5, was originally named "Muir's Peak" by famed naturalist John Muir, who loved not only the area, but the mountain, and spent days and nights alone near its peak, reveling in its beauty. In 1874 he wrote in his journal, "When I first caught sight of Shasta, I was fifty miles away and afoot, alone and weary. Yet all my blood turned to wine and I have not been weary since. Go where you may, there stands before you the colossal cone of Shasta, clad in ice and snow, the one grand unmistakable landmark — the pole star of the landscape."

In 1894 Muir wrote,"Would it not be a fine thing to set it apart for the welfare and benefit of all mankind, preserving its fountains and forests and all its glad life in primeval beauty?"

Clarence King is credited with discovering the glaciers on Mt. Shasta in the year 1870. However, we cannot overlook the fact that a man named I. S. Diehl mentioned the glaciers when he made his solo climb in in 1855.

It has always been affirmed that there are five glaciers on Mt. Shasta, and they are found side by side, forming an almost continuous covering for that portion of the mountain at an altitude of about 10,000 feet: Whitney glacier, named in honor of Professor Josiah Dwight Whitney, the noted scientist; Bolam glacier, which is an Indian name meaning "great"; Hotlum glacier, which is an Indian name meaning "steep rock"; Wintun glacier, which is an Indian tribal name; and Konwakiton, which is an Indian name meaning "dirty or muddy."

But the late Harry Watkins of Mount Shasta, who was untiring in his efforts to explore the glaciers, came up with some surprising facts; he maintained that there are eight, not five glaciers on the mountain.

"The belief that Mt. Shasta has only five glaciers," he said in an interview, "is a most persistent one. People do not seem to realize that many changes have occurred in the glaciers since 1885 when the first surveys of the mountain were completed, and that changes have also occurred in definition of what constitutes a glacier."

According to Watkins, the fact that there are more than five glaciers had also been confirmed by Mark F. Meier, a glaciologist with the United States Geological Survey group. Meier recognized eight glaciers on Mt. Shasta and said that the United States Glacier Survey map showed all of the glaciers very accurately, but continued to give names for only five, which served to perpetuate the belief that only five glaciers exist on the mountain.

What are glaciers? Glaciers are actually rivers of solid ice; they're like giant chisels and they carve deep ditches in the earth they move. Glaciers move, it's as simple as that. The basic difference between an ordinary ice field and a true glacier is the latter is moving, and because of this constant movement glaciers play an important role in sculpturing Mt. Shasta. Volcanoes are not composed of very solid rock and on a volcano like Mt. Shasta, which is built of hundreds of individual lava streams and layers of fragmental material which offer little resistance to glacial scouring, the glaciers are

Black Butte, which looms alongside Interstate 5, was originally named "Muir's Peak" by famed naturalist John Muir.

effective eroding agents. Powerful and relentless, a glacier can enter a winding valley, dig into its valley walls, and change its contour.

Experts say a glacier doesn't necessarily require snowfalls of enormous depth. What glaciers need is many cool summers during which the last winter's snowpack doesn't entirely melt. And the Mt. Shasta area is noted for its cool summers.

Many people, not familiar with the terrain of Mt. Shasta, are seemingly unaware of Mt. Shasta's glaciers, the largest in California. They are also unaware of the waterfalls, pastoral meadows, wild flowers, dwarf forests of trees presumed to be over 200 years old, and other natural phenomenon hidden on this great mountain. Whitney Falls, Coquette Falls, Lake Helen, Sisson Lake, Clarence King Lake, golden dome rocks and vast canyons are only a few of the attractions to be found by those who love the mountain's splendor.

Those immense glaciers have lain for centuries in Mt. Shasta's awesome gorges and they remain, for the most part, in secret solitude in their icy beds.

How did Mt. Shasta get its name?

The fact is, no one really knows for sure. Historians are indefinite about the naming of Mt. Shasta. Some say it was derived from the French word "chaste" which means pure, and some think it was a deviation from the Russian word "tsisti" meaning pure and white (Russian trappers came to the mountain from the coast in the early

1800s), and others think it came from an obscure Indian word used by native tribes, which could have been adopted by early white travelers through northern California.

In 1827 Peter Skeene Ogden, trapper and fur trader with the Hudson Bay Company, wrote in his journal: "There is a mountain of equal height to Mount Hood. I have named it Mount Sastise. I have given these names from the tribes of Indians." (He also named a river Sastise.) However, in later entries he spelled the name of the mountain "Sasty" or "Sastice" and his journal does not make clear which peak he named. Therefore, his journal entries have always been controversial. Dr. C. Hart Merriam's journal (Washington D. C. Academy of Science, XIV, 522 ff.) contains the reference that Peter Skeene Ogden referred to Mount McLoughlin and the Rogue River in Oregon, and he said the maps of the 1830s support this belief.

From the Henry Eld journal (Wilke's Overland Expedition to California with Lieutenant George Emmons in command) which Hugh F. Scanlon (1968 *Siskiyou Pioneer*, Vol. 4, No. 1) located in the Coe Collection at Yale University, comes a sketch-map dated October 4, 1841, which shows the group's first crossing of the Sacramento River — named Destruction River on the map — and which designates Mt. Shasta as "Sasty Peak".

A few years later, in 1844, another explorer with the unlikely name Duflot de Mofra drew up a map and put the mountain and the river in California, but his name for them was Mont Saste and R. des Sastes.

Four years later, early maps such as Fremont-Preuss printed "Mt. Tsashtl" and in 1852 Horn's Overland Guide used the name Shaste for Oregon's Rogue River.

An explorer named Brewster came through in 1862. He wrote in his journal that an Indian had pronounced the name of the mountain as "Tachasta" and since he had noticed on earlier maps the names Chasty, Brewster thought Tachasta was the native pronunciation. But he also thought there was a connection in the naming of the mountain to a tribe of Indians of Oregon.

And there have even been maps which named the peak Mount Jackson. Then an early settler named Gibbs said the Indian name for the mountain was "Wy-e-kah" and another tribe called the mountain "Bo-lem-poi-yok" which meant high peak. Add to this the fact that there really was a tribe of Shasta Indians whose summer encampment was beside Big Springs (still flowing in the city of Mount Shasta's park) but when Peter Skeene Ogden asked them the name of the nearby white mountain, their answer was, "He who sleeps in the clouds."

Towards the middle of the last century, an assemblyman from the Sacramento district proposed calling the county situated about 60 miles below the mountain "Shasta County" and following that, the mountain was referred to as "Shasta" on Scholfields' map of 1851. Some of the other maps of the 1850s refer to the mountain as Shasta Butte or Mount Shasta. Which brings up a point: Mt. Shasta is not spelled out as Mount Shasta in the immediate area of the mountain (particularly by journalists and writers) and the reason is to differentiate between Mt. Shasta, the mountain, and Mount Shasta, the colorful city which lies on the southwest base of the mountain.

Mount Shasta developed late in the last century as the logging industry grew, and through the years has developed a unique personality. In spite of its alpine rurality, the settlement has become a Mecca for sports enthusiasts, artists, professional people, naturalists, and various religious sects and cults who claim to be tuned in to the mystic vibrations found on the slopes of Mt. Shasta.

Three miles away is Lake Siskiyou, secluded and jewel-like, surrounded by evergreens. The area also provides skiing, both downhill and Nordic, as well as great hunting and fishing.

Within walking distance of the city is the Mount Shasta Fish Hatchery, established in 1888 and the oldest operating trout hatchery in California. The hatchery is a tourist attraction because visitors are allowed to view, in operation, the plant which raises millions of salmon and trout each year.

The city of Mount Shasta is a natural stopping-off place for thousands of weary, urban travelers who long for the solitude of the area's sky-touching pines and the spectacular view of one of the most enchanting mountains in the world. Silhouetted against a rose-tinged sky and always shrouded in mystery, Mt. Shasta's peak fills the northern California sky with beauty.

And native Mount Shastans still observe the snowy pinnacle with wonder from fragrant meadows far below.

Clarance King Lake, top of Shastina, turquoise in color. Summer. Photo by James E. Kottinger.

Whitney Creek Falls — dropping from a basalt (marble-like) canyon below Whitney Glacier. Summer. Photo by James E. Kottinger.

Golden dome-like rocks, probably caused from crusted sulphur, on the slopes of Mt. Shasta. Could be the source of the golden minarets and temples spotted from afar. Summer. Photo by James E. Kottinger.

Ancient weather beaten trees on lower slopes of Mt. Shasta.
Photo by James E. Kottinger.

Opposite Page: A lower meadow of Mt. Shasta's alpine belt. A quiet land above timberline.
This belt is easily accessed during snow free periods.
photo by Ed Stockton

Chapter 27

The Kingdom Of Shasta

Books have been written

about the various

mysteries of

Mt. Shasta,

and the mountain has

attracted curious people

from all over the

world.

High above, in the mist-shrouded forests and glistening peaks of Mt. Shasta, an air of mystery will always linger. But what about this internationally famed mountain, aside from its legends and mysteries?

Dramatically beautiful, Mt. Shasta is one of the largest stratovolcanoes in the world. This ever-white mountain rises to an altitude of 14,162 feet and its volume is said to be just over 80 cubic miles. Rising, as it does, directly and abruptly from the surrounding countryside, Shasta's kingdom lies far below, and is none other than wildly scenic Siskiyou County, keystone of the northern tier of California counties.

Countless ages ago nature performed a feat which is peculiar to our part of the world. The upheaval which formed California's western mountains played a delightful trick here. The valleys in Shasta's then-kingdom were peculiar in that they had no natural outlet except through steep, rugged canyons. Which meant, in days of old, that beautiful valleys were rimmed by high and almost impassable mountains with just a few natural passes. And so this irregular topography isolated Shasta's kingdom for centuries and seemingly prevented man's appearance until comparatively recent times.

It has been said the first crossing of the Siskiyou mountains was recorded in 1826 in an animal-skin diary kept by a Hudson Bay trapper who descended into what is now Shasta Valley.

Shasta's kingdom, known 164 years later as Siskiyou County, is big and sprawling, with evergreens as far as the eye can behold. It is California's most spectacular, most mountainous county, fifth largest in the state, and it lies approximately midway on the Pacific Coast. Bounded on the west by Del Norte and Humboldt counties, on the east by Modoc county and on the south by Shasta and Trinity counties, it borders the state of Oregon for about 110 miles.

The origin of the word "Siskiyou" has never been authentically determined. It was once thought that Siskiyou was the Indian name for a bob-tailed horse, but there is another story regarding its derivation and meaning. Senator Jacob R. Snyder of San Francisco, who advocated the formation of the county in 1852, stated that the French name "Six Callieux" was given to a ford on Oregon's Umpqua River at which place Michel La Frambeau (who led a party of Hudson Bay trappers) crossed in the year 1832. Six large stones lay in the river where they crossed and they gave it the name "Six Callieux" (meaning six-stone ford) and it is from this incident, some historians think, the Siskiyou mountains were later named and also California's northernmost county.

Siskiyou County is almost 70 miles wide and has an area of 4,043,710 acres — or 6,313 square miles — and is larger than the combined areas of Connecticut and Rhode

Island. But 60% is under public ownership (public ownership, of course, meaning the government).

The Klamath National Forest alone takes up over one million acres. Also included in this vast county are portions of the Shasta-Trinity, Rogue, Modoc and Six Rivers National Forests, not to mention the fabled Marble Mountain Wilderness Area.

Approaching Siskiyou County from the south, the traveler winds up the gorge of the Sacramento River. To the west, the peak of Mount Eddy reaches 9,038 feet. Westward, and almost equidistant upward, extend the Scott and Salmon mountains, drained by rivers of the same name which flow northerly and westerly into that famed trout and steelhead stream, the Klamath River.

A very old photo showing the Sacramento River much as the Indians knew it, as it flowed swiftly down the canyon below Castella. There's no prettier countryside anywhere than the Sacramento River in the springtime.

Northward, the Shasta River also winds down to the Klamath River, which flows from the Klamath Lakes in the northwestern corner of Siskiyou County and southern Oregon.

The headwaters of California's legendary river of gold, the Sacramento River, can be found high on Mount Eddy, and in the southeastern section of the county is that rare fishing stream, the McCloud River, home of the Dolly Vardon trout. The Scott River, reminiscent of the gold rush, runs from the high Trinity Divide northward to join the Klamath near the village of Happy Camp.

Ah, the Kingdom of Shasta, truly a wonderland. The spectacular Salmon-Trinity Alps in the southwestern corner are tipped with snow most of the year. Gold rush buildings are still to be seen in many quaint towns and Lotta Crabtree sang in some of them. Most of the old structures have changed little since they held crowds of miners suddenly wealthy with gold dust. Poet Joaquin Miller spent a winter mining for gold along Humbug Creek and told about it in a book. And, too, the kingdom contains the Lava Beds National Monument, stark battlegrounds where 70 half-starved Modoc Indians once held off United States cavalry troopers in a valiant effort to survive. (They didn't).

The Klamath is a river of many moods. Sometimes it's a wide, smooth stream and sometimes its course is marked by rapids and fierce currents. And then, sometimes it meanders leisurely through very picturesque countryside.

The Kingdom of Shasta is, because of its isolation, still aesthetically divine, with hundreds of miles of evergreen forests, whitewater rivers, secluded alpine lakes, misty waterfalls, mineral springs, fields of grain. It is Lake Siskiyou, Lake

Lake Siskiyou, three miles from the city of Mount Shasta. Mt. Eddy is shown above as it can be seen today from Interstate5. Named after Nelson Harvey Eddy, one of the earliest pioneers to the area who built a log cabin on the mountain's slopes in 1855

Lake McCloud, with its heavily forested banks. Locals may refer to this lake as McCloud Reservoir

Lake Shastina and the "Valley of a Thousand Hills"

High in the sky is Castle Lake. Deep blue and serene, it lies in the piney shadows of a cirque basin and covers about 47 acres. And there's a campground there.

There are many alpine lakes in this area. Pictured is icy Little Castle Lake, just a short hike above Castle Lake.

Medicine Lake is a hidden paradise for those who love the back country. Though this was once volcanic country, the lake is rimmed with trees.

Tule Lake Basin which lies on the major western Pacific Flyway.

Lava Beds petroglyphs found in Lava Beds National monument, near Mt. Shasta — the writings are of undetermined origin.
 Photo by James E. Kottinger

McCloud, Lake Shastina, Castle Lake (highest alpine lake) and myriads of hidden lakes. It is Glass Mountain, a gigantic mass of jet black obsidian which glistens and sparkles in the sun. It is Pumice Stone Mountain, and the Medicine Lake Highland. It is the Tule Lake Basin which lies on the major western Pacific Flyway, where in the spring and fall the sky becomes clouded with hundreds of thousands of birds and waterfowl. It is emerald meadows and rolling hills. It is sky-line lakes and deep blue sub-alpine lakes nestled in dense stands of lodgepole pines. It is skiing on Mt. Shasta's slopes in crystal air that angels breathe. It is nature displaying her handicraft through a million eras.

The ancient Klamath mountains loom westward from Mt. Shasta, across historic Strawberry Valley. Northeasterly, the Goosenest mountain range rises, and stretching along the northern border of Siskiyou County are the high, timbered ridges of the Siskiyou range.

As anyone can see, the Kingdom of Shasta is a land of mountains. And standing tallest of all in this domain of rugged, unbelievably beautiful ranges and peaks is magical, mystical Mt. Shasta, rising perennially white and solitary and serene — an ethereal, majestic sentinel guarding her kingdom.

In conclusion, this book would not be complete without the acknowledgement of my good friend, the late Austrian-born Edward Stuhl — naturalist, artist and avid conservationist. I am certain Stuhl loved the mountain more than anyone, ever, living or dead. Other great mountain men (John Muir, Clarence King, Joaquin Miller, William Bridge Cooke, Harry Watkins, Mac Olberman and others) have, indeed, left their mark on Mt. Shasta in one way or another, but the most magnificent love-gift of all to the mountain is Stuhl's collection of wildflower paintings, a project which spanned 25 years of his life. Of the 207 wildflower species known to grow on Mt. Shasta, he painted 204 of them. The other three species are up there somewhere, but he was never able to find them. As for the others, sometimes he had to wait years in order to find a certain wildflower at the exact right moment of bloom.

Stuhl lived to see his paintings preserved in a book, *Wildflowers of Mount Shasta, Lone Giant of the Cascades* which was compiled by Marilyn Clement Ford and can be purchased in Mount Shasta stores. The book also contains highlights of his journal written during his 67-year love affair with Mt. Shasta.

Edward F. Stuhl passed on in 1984 at the age of 97 but he lives on in his vivid journal entries, one of which I have chosen to close this book. It concerns his first view of Mt. Shasta in the summer of 1917.

Stuhl was 30 years old and his life took a very dramatic turn when he made his first trip to northern California. After a train ride to Redding, he proceeded to hike the 60-odd miles up to Mt. Shasta. Just below the spires of Castle Crags, in a bend in the Sacramento River canyon, the white peaks of Mt. Shasta came into full view. His sense of awe is revealed in his journal entry dated June 30th:

"I was surprised by one of the grandest sights I have ever beheld. There it rose above the canyon, framed by dark forest hillsides, bathed in sunlight. Was it a mirage or a beguiling upbuilding of rose-tinged, silvery-edged clouds? A vision suspended in mid-air? I doubted its reality, but it truly was Mt. Shasta.

"Awed and spellbound, I settled on a rock by the way-side and let the knapsack slip from my shoulder to the ground. I rested and looked and wondered. I felt as I had when I first saw the Adriatic Sea from the height of the Karst plateau as I watched the sun set into her golden flood — I felt as I did as a schoolboy when I walked over the Bavarian plain and greeted the Stubaier Alps from Tyrol. Those are impressions which settle deep.

"And now I sit in California at the foot and in the spell of Shasta. Old dreams and new longings arise — the love for a mountain by a stray mountaineer and the restless impulse for adventure and conquest. I will conquer this mountain."

Stuhl was one of the first people to ski on Mt. Shasta.

Emilie and Ed Stuhl overlooking his book Wildflowers of Mt. Shasta, Lone Giant of the Cascades.

Bibliography

CALIFORNIA BELL LEGEND: Vol. IV, No. 1, California Folklore Quarterly, January, 1945. Published by University of California at Los Angeles.

LEMURIA — LOST CONTINENT OF THE PACIFIC; By Wishar S. Cerve, Rosicrucian Press, Ltd., San Jose, California.

UNVEILED MYSTERIES; By Godfre Ray King, published by the Saint Germain Press, Chicago, Illinois.

THE SISKIYOU PIONEER: Vol. 2, No. 4, 1953, published by the Siskiyou County Historical Society, Yreka, California. Also Vol. 1, No. 1, 1946.

LORD MAITREYA, or THE NEW GOLDEN AGE: By Mah-Atmah Amsumata (Norman R. Westfall), published by the Amsumata Publishing Co. Shrine Temple, Los Angeles, California.

MYSTERIES OF MOUNT SHASTA: By M. Doreal, published by the Brotherhood of the White Temple, Inc., Sedalia, Colorado.

LOST MINES AND HIDDEN TREASURES: By Leland Lovelace, 1956, published by The Naylor Company, San Antonio, Texas 78296.

THE GOLDEN GODDESS OF THE LEMURIANS: By Abraham Mansfield, 1970, published by Abraham Mansfield, Redding, California.

A DWELLER ON TWO PLANETS: By Frederick Spencer Oliver, who claimed Phylos the Tibetan "dictated" the book and was the true author. Published in 1940 by Borden Publishing Company, Los Angeles, California.

THE LOST CONTINENT OF MU: By Colonel James Churchward.

THE STORY OF ATLANTIS AND THE LOST LEMURIA By W. Scott-Elliot.

FIRE and ICE — THE CASCADE VOLCANOES: By Stephen L. Harris, 1976, published by The Mountaineers, Pacific Search Books, Seattle, Washington. Revised edition, 1988:

FIRE MOUNTAINS of the WEST — THE CASCADES AND MONOLAKE VOLCANOES by Stephen L. Harris, published by the Mountain Press Publishing Co., Missoula, Montana.

KLAMATH FALLS HERALD & NEWS; Lee Juillerat piece, 9/27/81

ENCYCLOPAEDIA BRITANNICA: 1954 Edition, Vol,14 (re: Lemuria)